STUPID, EVIL, *or* **BOTH**

A COLLECTION OF RANTS

Ranted by: Radic Allef Tist

ISBNs

Paperback (Amazon KDP): 979-8-9999058-3-3

Paperback (Ingram): 979-8-9999058-6-4

EPUB: 979-8-9999058-7-1

PDF: 979-8-9999058-4-0

Others I haven't used (literally cheaper to buy ten at once, go figure):

979-8-9999058-0-2

979-8-9999058-1-9

979-8-9999058-2-6

979-8-9999058-5-7

979-8-9999058-8-8

979-8-9999058-9-5

First Edition: September 2025

Publisher: Progress Foundry LLC

DISCLAIMER

This book is a work of critical commentary, personal opinion, and expressive speech. It contains strong language, direct criticism, and emotionally charged assessments of public figures, organizations, institutions, and widely covered events. The tone is unapologetically subjective, and the content is intended as a reflection of the author's views and interpretations — not as an objective or neutral account.

This book references real people, organizations, and verifiable events, many of which are drawn from public records, mainstream news, or other publicly accessible sources. The author has made reasonable efforts to ensure factual accuracy where applicable. However, readers should understand that this book is not a work of journalism or investigative reporting. It is an exercise of personal speech, protected under the First Amendment of the United States Constitution and other applicable free speech laws.

Harsh language, metaphors, insults, and other provocative phrasing used throughout are intended as rhetorical devices, emotional expression, or satire. Unless explicitly supported and presented as factual, such statements should not be interpreted as literal accusations or verifiable claims. The author disclaims any defamatory intent and does not aim to cause harm to the reputation of any person or entity.

Any opinions expressed about public figures or institutions are based on the author's personal perspectives and interpretations of publicly known actions, statements, or behaviors. The inclusion of any name or likeness does not imply endorsement, agreement, or factual wrongdoing unless specifically and clearly stated.

This book does not provide legal, medical, financial, psychological, or professional advice. It is not intended to guide readers' actions or substitute for professional consultation. The author disclaims all liability for any decision made by a reader based on the content of this work.

All rights to commentary, critique, parody, artwork, and expressive opinion are reserved. Readers are encouraged to engage critically and form their own views.

TABLE OF CONTENTS

INTRODUCTION

AMERICAN CONSERVATISM IS STUPID, EVIL, OR BOTH

That's it. That's the premise of the book.

You overpaid, trust-fund baby propagandists over at Fox, OANN, Newsmax, and all the other echo chambers can slap that title up in your favorite color on your "news" shows and cry about why opinions like mine aren't being censored while your free speech is under attack. Though if you read ahead, I have no doubt you'll find many more little blurbs for you to take out of context. As you so love to do.

But yes, that is the subject of this book. It's a long rant — or really a collection of long rants — about right-wing American Conservative ideology, its foolish, disastrous, short-sighted, hypocritical, corrupt, greedy, wicked policies, and the failures of the people that support them.

This isn't called "Stupid, Evil, or Both: A Psychological Evaluation of the Conservative Ethos: A Super Scientific Socioeconomic Study: With Thousands of References to Accredited Peer-Reviewed Journals: A New York Times Bestseller". It's not going to be that fancy.

Here, this is the only chart that'll be in the whole book:

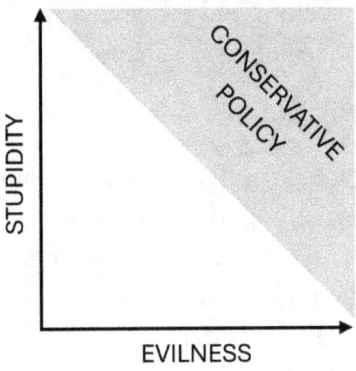

Figure 1. An illustration showing the placement of all
American Conservative policy on the Stupid-Evil Scale

When I say "Conservatives" all throughout this book, I'm talking about both the passive and active supporters of right-wing platforms, and more specifically *American* Conservatives — From the sweet old lady in your suburb that's faithfully voted Republican all her life, all the way to the raging MAGA zealots that stormed our Capitol.

Some Conservatives are not inherently evil. They go about life blissfully unaware of anything going on, possessing little to no understanding of the way anything works, what the policy issues are, or how their vote impacts the society they think is just wonderful.

They treat everyone in their sphere of influence with kindness and love, then tribalistically vote for Team R because that's what they think they're supposed to do.

These sorts of people might even be brilliant in their own way! Like how an astrophysicist or a neurosurgeon can still be totally ignorant about anything but space or brains. This is a common form of Conservative — the kind that supports them through a thoughtless vote alone. But thoughtless support is still support.

Some Conservatives are extraordinarily malicious and also highly intelligent, having full sociopathic awareness of the impact and damage of their policies. They often wildly enrich themselves through the pain and suffering they cause, seeking only to amass their wealth and influence through carefully calculated schemes.

They use their gifts for evil, and they don't care who gets hurt.

This is the rarest form of Conservative, because Conservatism in the U.S. is, fundamentally, a vastly ignorant ideology. However, this is the kind of person that doesn't really care about all that and simply votes for the team that will carry them to noteworthy power and unfathomable wealth. Pesky morals and ethics be damned.

And then there's everything else in the triangle.

INTRODUCTION

<u>ABOUT THE BOOK</u>

The idea with this book is that I'll have a general topic for each section with some sub-categories sprinkled in where relevant. I'll rant for a while in each section like you give a shit, and then maybe give my thoughts on how things might be fixed or what Progressive policy dreams are out there. Pretty simple.

There is no reason for the order, no hierarchy of importance, no real pattern. Just topics of interest, the ways American policies suck, and how Conservatives vote to keep it that way or make it all worse.

As of this moment, here during my probably terribly done self-editing, it is about six months into the tangerine tyrant's second term. The fascism has only just begun brewing. It may be in full swing before I finish the drafts, get the manuscript fully edited, and start the publishing process. Point is, by the time this book is out there, I've probably missed a lot of depressing news.

That said, this book is attacking U.S. Conservatism as an ideology, not *just* highlighting current events. This is a commentary on the U.S. Conservative platform as much as it is a blunt criticism of the people that support it.

I'm obviously from the United States, but the right-wing, nationalist, regressive ideologies U.S. Conservatives espouse exist all around the globe, so there will be times when the ranting has a measure of international relevance.

I know that "Conservative" doesn't mean the same thing everywhere around the world and that many nicer country's Conservatives are actually the good guys. Just imagine whatever party has the most idiotic and comically malicious policies in your country — that's who I mean. In America, it's our Conservatives — usually of the Republican Party.

I'm not really eloquent enough to write deep, thoughtful essays on all the ways Conservative policy ruins everything. I'm just fucking mad and wrote my anger down. I needed to organize my rage in a constructive way and decided this book could be a distracting means of doing that while sharing my frustrations with the world.

ABOUT THE RANTER

While I personally place very little value on my own self-worth, I do appreciate context. Knowing what sort of person is ranting throughout this book is an important detail to consider. If I was some billionaire's kid living on a luxury yacht, I wouldn't listen to me either.

I'm a millennial (shocker), with a mom and dad that are caricatures of your typical Boomer mentality, outlook, and general understanding of why the world is the way it is. They've both voted Republican their whole life and have therefore supported the development of the problems I'm ranting about. I have to imagine many others have parents just like mine.

I won't go much into my mom, because I do love her and I understand that her views on politics are mostly born of ignorance. Fox was the only "news" my dad watched. She fits into the set of Conservatives that I'd probably call "most easily forgiven". The sort that doesn't actively have a lot of hate in their heart, they just never knew much better and fell for the disinformation Fox uses regularly.

They didn't *really* think about what they were voting for beyond Team R. Their vote counted just as much as everyone, yes, but it's that faint glimmer of hope that they could possibly come around to see reason that keeps you from being irreparably pissed at them. Like the sweet old suburb lady.

INTRODUCTION

I know some would argue that the people in this bucket are worse in some way — to be so careless about something as vital as your vote. I get that, for sure. But these are the people that can be shown a new, better way and can be converted to the light side. We can hope, anyway.

Then there's my dad. This slew of rants could basically be directed right at him. You couldn't paint a better picture of the type of person I'm so angry at when discussing the state of the country.

He grew up privileged and well-off, was rescued by numerous bailouts and handouts from his war-veteran father, and was gifted a pile of inheritance big enough to erase all debts, kill off all fiscal anxieties, and grace him with a fairly early retirement.

Yet he insists he had no privilege, that he worked for and earned everything, and that my clueless Progressive views will ruin any shot I have at financial freedom. He has watched my own financial struggles with apathy while dangling a very modest inheritance over me.

He's that kind of ironically brown-skinned racist that lets it slip in ways from light comments to full-on hard R-ing while quietly reading the news on the couch, despite he himself looking like a minority. He claims to not care about gay or trans people, but still argues that the Constitution says they shouldn't have rights. He spews conspiratorial bullshit about every Democrat's crimes, but of course thinks the Mons Olympus-worth of Republican crimes are fake.

You get the idea, probably because this caricature is so disturbingly common in this country. There's so much more I could say, but I'll let this wordy book paint that picture and save the rest for therapy. If I can afford it.

Anyway, as for me, I was born and raised in fucking Texas, unfortunately. I grew up in a fairly average house — nothing high-class about it. I had odd jobs for extra cash, but mostly focused on school and various extracurriculars.

I would've described myself as a Republican when I was younger. I also called myself a Christian. Wore the cross necklace and everything. Indoctrination and peer pressure at a young age does that, though I am now firmly agnostic.

It wasn't until a couple of years into college that I really shifted how I identified myself.

Social media was just beginning to blossom in popularity at that time. The internet itself was exploding with possibility and access to information was on a logarithmic ride upwards. All I had growing up was my dad blaring Fox News too. I remember hearing him scream at the TV about Clinton doing things, how dumb he thought the Democrats were, etc. etc.

But when I mentally developed enough for deeper introspection and was able to take advantage of the wealth of information the internet had to offer, it did not take long for me to see how utterly shit my parents' "team" was, and how right-wing priorities and platforms were completely conflicted with my values and character.

You see, all I had to do was start actually paying attention to the goings-on of the world instead of voting for the "team" my parents rooted for.

The university didn't tie me to the desk and hypnotize me with Liberal programming to add another convert to their ranks. I was *always* a gentle, kind, empathetic person. I just, regretfully, didn't give mind to politics until I was college-age. It was a little harder to do in a small suburban Red-state town before the internet really took off.

My point is that I grew. More importantly, I *out*grew the foolish and wicked viewpoints embedded in the Conservative mindset that surrounded me and my life. I realized that I never actually agreed with anything Republicans were saying or doing, and I only called myself Republican out of ignorant allegiance and the ramblings of my dad shitting on Democrats all my life.

INTRODUCTION

I'm just glad I became self-aware sooner rather than later.

I also think awareness of my current financial situation gives pretty necessary context when considering everything in this book —

My undergraduate degree was paid for almost entirely by money from my grandfather (yes, on my dad's side) and a large pile of scholarships. I had great grades, yet the combination of a rough job market, a pinch of disillusionment, a sprinkling of depression, and a crippling dearth of self-confidence sent me down career path I later regretted.

I eventually went back to school for a master's degree as a sort of "reset", which I paid for myself with federal student loans and a simple job while in school.

I now make middle-class money. My partner, who is still working on their degree due to their own parents' shortcomings, makes very little. We are able to save some, but not enough that an emergency or broken appliance wouldn't set us back many months or more. I also own my home — well, a mortgage — only thanks to Covid-era interest rates.

The point is I'm doing fine, better than many, but I still anxiously budget and fret about our financial future.

Unlike my father, I recognize the privilege given to me. I don't pretend like I had no help, and I am very grateful for the blessings I do have. I know that so many people don't have that luxury or even a safety net to rely on, through no fault of their own.

In summary, I am just some mostly-white, middle-class, unremarkable person. I have made many regrettable choices. I have many personal faults. I have negligible self-confidence and am highly critical of myself. I'm empathetic enough to care about this stuff, but not enough to fight the paradox of intolerance.

I'm smart enough to see how little I know. Dumb enough to prove it with this book.

It took me a few weeks to write the first draft, but it took me much, much longer to do the editing and the artwork (I know it sucks — I used free software, the print quality was disappointing, and I'm very much *not* an artist or graphic designer). Plenty has already happened, and even more will happen before this book is published.

I am not an expert on anything in here. I recognize that I have as much credibility as some rando off the street. My statistics will be generalized. I'll likely miss some nuance. My solutions to problems might be their own flavor of stupidity. My understanding of some topics may be too broad to be taken seriously.

I will forget to mention some things. I will purposefully ignore talking about some things because of my profound ignorance regarding said things. I will rant too long about some things.

I really can't stress enough that I'm just pissed off and this is a book I'm writing as a kind of self-therapy. This is not a comprehensive analysis, it's a wall of criticism. I'm bitching in book form.

Maybe you're a Democrat/Progressive/Leftist looking for a good ol' circle-jerk of opinions. Maybe you're a Republican/Conservative/Right-winger looking for more things to hate and add to your bonfire queue.

Regardless, this book is more for me to complain and vent my perspective than it is an attempt to rally like-minded Progressives or sway uncertain Conservatives.

I don't expect it to go anywhere far either. This book ain't Romantacy, so it's not about making money. I just felt like getting my thoughts out there and I charged enough to make a few bucks per book, but nothing egregious. Printing costs are kind of nuts, apparently. Especially color.

I chose to publish this anonymously for safety, but I probably fucked up somewhere and it might eventually come out who I am. I'd get the usual flood of online outrage, the calls for punishment, legal threats, and maybe even some real-life harassment or worse. Let's just say I wouldn't be worried about my life if this book was criticizing Progressives. And plenty of those books exist.

Sharing your opinions on politics at all these days is a risk.

I know that it's selfish of me to invite all that worry to my family, but my partner still supports me doing this. They know how much I've needed to put into words the disgust I feel with a significant swath of people in this country, or really this world.

It rattles around in my head, builds pressure like a giant pissed-off magma chamber, and erupts in short bursts of volcanic anger when my dad regurgitates the latest right-wing slop.

I need to share my feelings. I need an atypical therapeutic outlet, and this is the best personality fit I can think up.

So anyway, thanks for reading even just this much.

Let's begin.

OUR VOTE

OUR VOTE

In other countries, political nuances are allowed to exist. You can have multiple parties that may be mostly similar aside from a few key issues, and voters are able to give democratic power to those distinctions.

In the U.S. political spectrum, it might be prudent to separate the "conservative Democrats" from the "liberal Democrats" so people know how they might lean on Progressive party goals.

No such distinction is really required for today's Republicans, of course. They are all Conservatives, but the question becomes more about how extreme they are. Are they calmer, country club Ivy League Heritage Foundation Republicans or the screeching loyalists of the MAGA herd?

Unfortunately for us Americans, the nuance is utterly meaningless. Our voting systems and the finances behind them ensure that it just doesn't fucking matter.

You vote for a single platform from one of two parties regardless of how respectable or horrendous a candidate is, and our disastrously anti-democratic, corporation-owned voting systems and campaign finance laws guarantee you have no other real choice.

And then when it comes time for those legislators to actually represent *you* and why *you* voted for them, they instead vote straight down party lines 99% of the time. So many of these people don't even read the bills they vote for. They just check if a Republican or a Democrat wrote it and vote accordingly without any other analysis.

So that's it. You get to choose between the Republican candidate's platform or the Democratic candidate's platform and every other option is lost to the void of our "democracy".

THE REPUBLICAN PLATFORM

Well then what *is* the Republican platform? What do they stand for?

Republicans champion limited government and personal freedoms, to remove federal overreach, and strengthen States' rights.

But what they vote for is to be involved in everything you do, from your bedroom to your classroom.

They fight to control who you can marry, what you do with your body, what books you're allowed to read, and what religion you're exposed to.

They demonize as many marginalized groups as their base can remember, reaching for someone to blame for all their failings while claiming that social injustices are fiction.

They protect freedom of speech for Christian white nationalists, but not for the LGBTQ+ community or anti-fascists.

They demand States' rights, but only for States that will do the bidding of a Republican Fed.

Republicans vote for limited progressive government, not limited conservative government.

Republicans call for a market free from regulation, oversight, and government interference, where fundamental economic principles like supply and demand can decide the fate of businesses.

But what they vote for is to rig the game so their top donors flourish and smaller businesses suffocate.

They build a market landscape where oligarchs and the corporate elite can continue to exploit their workers and further widen the gap in wealth inequality through deregulation, union-busting, and the erosion of consumer protection law.

They install their own protectionist economic policies, like nonsense tariffs and corporate subsidies, to mandate a Republican agenda and pass the expense onto the poorest Americans.

They blind the prying eyes of the SEC and ethics committees to allow insider trading and crypto memecoin schemes.

They want companies free to abuse and rob their customers and employees without fear of legal retribution.

Republicans vote for a lawless market, not a healthy, fair one.

Republicans cry for less government spending and lower taxes.

But what they vote for is lighter burdens on those with wealth beyond reason and to force everyone else to cover the inevitable shortfalls.

They push for less government spending on projects Americans actually need while spending unaudited amounts on the combat arm of the military, corporate subsidies, and other self-enrichment ventures.

They burn through our tax dollars so the president can live on the golf course and dignitaries can lodge at his resorts.

They balloon the deficit every year they own it, and bitch about or block every Democratic effort to reduce it.

They directly cause the majority of economic recessions and worse through myopic, self-indulgent, and ultimately witless fiscal policy.

Republicans vote to rob money from those who need it the most and spend it on elitist goals, not to fund the people's true needs.

Republicans advocate for personal responsibility and a strong system of justice that's empowered to defend society and combat lawlessness.

But what they vote for is to fill their party with crooks, liars, grifters, and criminal scum.

They regularly elect brazenly corrupt, imbecilic, meritless people into the highest offices of the land.

They manufacture crimes from the most marginalized groups in the country and ignore or reward the heinous acts committed from within their own ranks.

They deploy a suffocating torrent of hypocrisy in the face of an adversary's supposed misconduct, then fall deathly silent or project new realities when the crimes are of their own.

They believe in a justice system that serves their fellows and the wealthy, rather than one that judges all equally.

Republicans vote for a convicted felon, alleged rapist, known racist, and serial conman, not law and order for all.

Republicans vow to support our brave countrymen and to honor their service and sacrifice to our nation.

But what they vote for is to gut veterans' benefits, to dismantle mental health and suicide-prevention programs, to end affordable housing incentives, and to privatize the VA.

They support our troops by perpetually keeping them at war to serve the energy giants and weapons manufacturers.

They support our troops by treating them as a big stick to be waved for economic leverage and to threaten our allies and neighbors.

They support our troops by slapping a red, white, & blue bumper sticker on their trucks and a blurb on their campaign webpages.

They support our troops like they're the unborn, by forgetting them when their political usefulness has been exhausted.

Republicans vote to abuse our troops as they do average Americans, not to support their health and wellness.

The real Republican platform is built by hypocrisy, hate, fear, and lies.

It relies on a deluge of gaslighting and propaganda, so truth becomes meaningless and new realities are born daily.

It obstructs justice to shield its members from any form of accountability for ethical transgressions to fully criminal acts.

It projects on others its own tower of inadequacies to deflect blame and shape a false image of its enemies.

It clutches a phony Christian identity to justify policies devoid of the very compassion and empathy demanded by the faith.

It pens laws that force women and young girls to carry and birth their rapist's baby.

It cripples the government and intentionally orchestrates its inefficacy, all to gain support for elite-friendly tax reform.

It seeks to revive both a thriving economic past without the taxes needed, and an ignoble social past rife with injustice and inequality.

It votes against reforms meant to help their constituents yet still takes credit for any progressive change that passes.

It enriches the wealthy few while harming the working many.

It provokes culture wars and a fear of the "other" to maintain control.

It exploits veterans and religion to ignite patriotic passions in a base conditioned to embrace tribalistic ideals without question.

It threatens to arrest rivals for playing the same political games its own party thrives on.

It prefers that the world burn and flood to admitting the truth of climate science and endeavoring to be better stewards of the planet.

It cries for meritocracy while employing and elevating the most incompetent, unqualified, clueless upward failures imaginable.

It devalues education and ignores experts while defunding research, extorting schools, and trying to rewrite history.

It feigns concern over a debt its own policies repeatedly inflates, while lambasting opponents who reduce it.

It blocks the public release of the Epstein client list to protect the pedophilic elite.

It imposes as much perplexing paperwork as possible for those applying for welfare, yet bemoans any such bureaucracy for businesses.

It views foreign aid as a tool for control and a waste of tax dollars rather than a humanitarian calling.

It obsesses with being anti-Progressive and damaging its enemies to the point of failing to do anything positive for the country.

It welcomes conspirators and insurrectionists among its ranks with pride.

It emboldens our longest-standing anti-democratic foreign enemies and economic rivals.

It blames the world's problems on the disenfranchised few instead of working to solve them with equality and inclusion.

It forces religious rules onto a land built around freedom of expression.

It elects a geriatric moronic monument to sin and would-be tyrannical king to lead and champion its vision.

It campaigns on limited government, yet flirts with the dream of fascism, a religious ethno-state, the consolidation of power and wealth, and the rapid erosion of checks and balances.

THAT is the platform represented every time the (R) is chosen at the ballot box. Every single election.

It is the platform lead by corrupted oligarchs, spineless sycophants, inept opportunists, immature bullies, shameless hypocrites, and serial liars. It is the platform that attracts authoritarians, white supremacists, warmongers, bigots, and other dangerous, ignorant idealogues.

Oh, but what about the enlightened people that vote Republican because they are "socially liberal" but "economically conservative"? Wow, you're so deep and nuanced! Good for you!

Setting aside how objectively interconnected those concepts are, what "economically conservative" Republican voters mean by this is that their money is more important to them than things like civil rights equality, corporate accountability, environmental protections, healthcare reform, and every other subject that impacts a scale greater than themselves.

Really though it's worse than that, because Republican policy so rarely puts more money in the wallets of regular people. They always *claim* they are decreasing taxes, and they might do that some marginal amount (especially if you're rich). But it's all a lie.

When your groceries, healthcare, childcare, education, utilities, simple pleasures, and fucking everything else in your life gets more expensive, your buying power plummets, and your financial future gets bleaker… then did you truly gain any money at all?

It's an *illusion!* They don't save you money!

Their "tax breaks" mantras are merely a means to further ease the burden for the wealthy. That's all there is to it.

Saying you are "economically conservative" only means you failed to notice how many different ways Conservative policy financially fucks you, and your empathy is frailer than your greed.

Now if you're exceptionally wealthy, then sure, choosing such an economic policy might make sense for you! But I'd wager most Conservative voters can't afford that country club membership.

When you vote Republican, you choose this platform and the sum of its parts to govern our future. You cannot vote for an economic platform without the attached social platform because we don't get that granular level of choice in our leaders. You decide which policies are most valuable to you and shape the legacy of our shared country.

And the legacy of the Republican platform is stupidity and evil.

THE DEMOCRATIC PLATFORM

So if the Republicans have the stupid, evil platform, that means the Democrats should be the fierce warriors of truth and benevolence, right? Haha right?

The fact is that while the Democrats *have* traditionally been a force for good, even progressive change in the country, there are still far too many old, conservative-leaning Democrats in office to enact the transformative Newer Deal change this country desperately needs.

It's the Me Generation Boomer dinosaurs clinging to their power and status, guzzling their corporation-backed campaign funds, and blocking bright, young Progressives from taking the reins. This Democratic Party is the same one caught organizing smear campaigns against their fellows so they could foist their own deeply unpopular candidate onto the ballot. Everyone saw that Hillary had the charisma of a spoiled potato.

Our Democrats would be seen as center-right in other countries. We have no true Progressive party, and our current system wouldn't ever allow for one to flourish.

We are stuck with the Democrats to fight evil — And they lose too frequently and capitulate too readily.

They have had full dominance of the government before — a few times even. I realize that legislation takes time, but why is it that when the Republicans take over, their team seems prepped and ready to implement a tsunami of unpopular, wicked, often illegal policies while the Democrats twiddle their thumbs or even reach across the aisle to join? Like when they vote to confirm Trump's disaster of a Cabinet.

You aren't supposed to stay friends and negotiate with fascists!

Each time the Dems held the majority, they *could* have voted in perfect lockstep with Progressive policy pushes. They *could* have implemented safeguards against people like Trump and his cronyism. They *could* have made real strides to reform the things that need it most.

They *could* have pushed to expand the courts, to pave the way for universal healthcare, to improve the federal minimum wage, to heavily increase taxes on the wealthy, to ban congressional stock trading, to make the poorest in our country healthier and happier, to make education more accessible than ever, to enshrine the freedom of choice for women, to protect the rights of marginalized communities, to make the government less corrupt and more democratic, and all the other policies I rant about in this stupid book.

They make little attempts at all of this here and there and sometimes celebrate small victories. But most of the efforts they make are not bold enough. They get stopped and blocked and voted down even by their own fellows. It feels like these Democrats do *just* enough to tell Progressives, "See? We are trying!"

Most of the old guard Democrats *like* their corporate money and insider trading. They *like* upholding the illusion of working for good without the colossal sacrifices necessary to *accomplish* that good. Being performative is so much easier than actually *doing* anything.

Look at how they behave when any Progressive wins a seat or even just attempts to gain political ground! They defend the status quo, not democracy. It's hard not to lump right-leaning Dems in with the worst — with everyone else I criticize in this angry book.

Now I'm not trying to discount the loads of Democrats in office that *are* trying to be forces for good. They are out there battling, challenging as much Republican fuckery as they can. You can watch them on C-SPAN being outspoken critics of Conservative stupidity and evil.

I feel for them, and I'd vote for their leadership in a heartbeat (assuming their voting record matches their bark). It must get exasperating to be constantly thwarted by your own party's fecklessness and stoicism in the face of a budding authoritarian regime.

The sad truth is that it will take a vast valley of gravestones before the influence of this Old Guard fades. Don't get all worked up, I just mean the Boomers have to pass on. Via time. Time takes us all. Anyway.

The only thing that will stop the rise of fascism is an opposing force both willing and strong enough to push back, and the current Democratic Party has proven several times that they are not an adequate force.

That doesn't mean they lose my vote, for now. The system we have won't allow me to vote any other way if I want to prevent stupidity and evil from taking charge.

The Democrats are, at the very least, the team that puts out the most good and tries to block as much Republican vitriol as they can.

I'm still furious with them, but do you blame the arsonists for starting the fires, or do you blame the firefighters that brought squirt guns instead of hoses?

OUR VOTING SYSTEMS

Our voting systems pretty intentionally cause this debilitating lack of choice. Two teams battling it out makes for great marketing, after all.

To start, first-past-the-post is the dumbest fucking way to do democracy. It is mathematically impossible for the system to output anything but two parties. Other folks can certainly throw their hat in and make some waves, but they will *always* be bound to the will of the largest groups.

Even if they got as much as 30% of the vote, their extent of representation and influence within the government would not even remotely reflect the share of votes they won.

And worse still, these third parties often do nothing but siphon support from the most like-minded main party. A highly progressive third-party candidate would irrefutably seize votes from Democratic candidates, which would only lead to Republican victory.

Imagine this — you've got three parties vying for leadership of the government. Republicans, Democrats, and let's call them Bernies.

The Bernies get 31% of the popular vote.

The Democrats get 34% of the popular vote.

The Republicans get 35% of the popular vote.

The Republicans win this election in our FPTP system — Despite the fact that Bernie progressive policy more closely aligns with the Democrats, *and* that 99% of the Bernie voters would pick Democrats with no other choice. That 65% combined majority is meaningless. It's so fucking stupid and not at all a representative democracy.

And it gets even worse when you look at the Electoral College.

There's a really good reason why it's usually only Republicans ever arguing to keep that shit system in place.

You can spin it any way you want, but in practice it means that the people living in the most populated areas have a fraction of the voting power and representation as those in some cornfield flyover Red state.

Why is it a-okay to eradicate the voting power of millions upon millions of densely populated urbanized states to coddle the sparsely populated rural plains?

Why do so many just shrug at the notion of "swing states" as if it makes total sense that these few places get more election attention than dozens of states combined?

Why is it just dandy that millions of citizens abstain from the democratic process because the Electoral College makes their vote feel worthless?

"Oh well I live in a [Red or Blue] state so my vote doesn't even count."

The Electoral College is a sham voting system and needs to be terminated right alongside FPTP.

The Red States wield plenty of powers at the state and local level to tackle the needs of their handful of citizens (as if Republican lawmakers actually care about their constituents lol).

Holding tens of millions of city-dwellers hostage is not the answer, especially when so many federal decisions affect the entire population regardless of your home state.

It somehow gets worse still when you look at gerrymandering!

Fucking Jackson Pollock-ass district lines everywhere.

Go look at some of the maps! These meticulously calculated divides are arranged to manipulate the voting blocs for specified outcomes.

What a convoluted disgrace, honestly. Just draw the lines evenly! Why are politicians getting to choose their voters instead of voters choosing their politicians?

All that gerrymandering does is allow a 48% Democrat state to only get 20% of the seats. And the same goes for Blue states and Republican voters! This should piss *everyone* off!

It is flabbergasting to me that this embarrassment hasn't changed for the better over the centuries.

There has been some push for states to agree that, regardless of the overall Electoral College result, their electoral votes will always go to the most popular candidate. That…helps I guess? But it really doesn't do anything to fix the underlying issues.

We need a complete overhaul of our voting systems.

🛠 HOW WE COULD FIX IT 🛠

I've thought about a few solutions over the years. The simplest change is a form of Ranked Choice voting where you rank your preferences by number and it does an automatic run-off system where the best overall "ranked" candidate wins. But that has a series of flaws too.

There is also a better, but more complicated system called Rated Voting where voters can give an approval rating to candidates, either by simple checkboxes or by some kind of numerical scale to indicate their approval score. The candidate with the most approval wins.

Either of those systems would be a titanic improvement over FPTP.

I had an idea myself about our ballots not having names or party affiliations on them at all but instead having a long list of statements about the policies, and the voter needs to decide how they feel about those policies.

It could be some kind of "greatly agree, somewhat agree, etc." scale, or maybe another numerical scale to show what this topic means to the voter and how it ranks to them.

The choices could even get more nuanced where voters select a preferred solution to a pressing issue. For example, all the candidates could agree that homelessness is a serious problem, and the ballot would have the candidates' policies to choose from without listing names.

Candidates will have answered all these same questions and scaled them to appropriately match their campaign.

Voters have now chosen what issues and policies they value the most, and even which solutions they prefer, and the victorious candidate will most closely align with what the majority chose. When the election ends, the candidates' choices are all made public and voters are now able to hold their representatives to their promises.

This is surely some kind of mathematical and logistical nightmare that has a million flaws, ignoring the fact that I'm asking people to actually read and think critically when they are at the ballot box.

My *point* was to somehow eliminate the aggravating tribalism in elections. Too many people circle a "team" instead of voting for how they actually feel, with little to no knowledge of the policies that the candidates truly stand for.

Anyway, once we change our methods of voting, then everyone needs ample opportunity *to* vote. Other countries even legally mandate that their citizens vote, with notable punishments for abstaining. I frankly wouldn't be opposed to that.

Before we get to that extreme though we can simply make voting more accessible to the everyday citizen.

Our country has no requirements for businesses to give paid-time-off for voting. It has poor voting access infrastructure. It has backwards voter registration laws with no same-day registration. It allows states to purge legally registered voters with little to no oversight or consequence for mistakes. It has notable limitations to early voting and mail-in voting.

Also, the voting period is far too short. Make it a week or a month or whatever amount of time is needed to ensure every single eligible voter has time to get to the polls and do their civic duty.

Our country puts excessive effort into making it as hard as possible to vote, and, go figure, it's chiefly Conservative policy looking to disenfranchise population centers, minorities, and anyone else that doesn't primarily vote R. We need to fix all of this.

For a nation so proud to be a democracy, we sure erect loads of barriers to its intended purpose.

And while we're at it, we should look at ending the use of voting machines/computers and return to paper ballots — or at least install as many safeguards as possible to make voting secure and accurate.

When an elected billionaire brags about how much his top billionaire donor knows about voting machines, it invites only conspiracies and distrust in the entire system.

And finally, gerrymandering needs to be eradicated.

Why are the leaders of any political party allowed to be involved in the map-drawing process at all? Why does the map-drawing process even need to be more complicated than separation by highway or some geographical feature?

Hell, they could just be fucking squares!

But no, Republicans will come in and draw maps that push *just* enough minority houses around so that a county goes Red for decades, and our ethically bankrupt Supreme Court says that's fair game.

This all means that the only way to fix this current two-party system is to fundamentally rewrite how we do voting. Easy, right?

Forsake FTTP, abolish the electoral college, incinerate gerrymandering maps, broaden voting accessibility, and do anything else that makes the way we vote more democratic and fairer.

Too bad both the parties in power are incentivized to preserve all this broken bullshit.

CITIZENS UNITED AND SUPER PACS

Citizens United — what a fucking phony name for what is one of, if not *THE,* most corruption-friendly Supreme Court rulings in existence. Guess who defends it tooth and nail?

It wasn't some grassroots alliance of citizens, it was (you guessed correctly) a Conservative nonprofit political organization called Citizens United that wanted to smear Hillary Clinton with some film in 2008. The FEC said that violated campaign finance law. Conservatives sued. And then the 2010 Supreme Court ruled 5-4 (down party lines) that political corruption was totes legal.

They said that "political spending is protected speech under the First Amendment." So corporations are now considered people for the purpose of free speech.

You hear that? The Supreme Court says that the more money you have, the more free speech you can have!

That stupid shit paved the way for Super PACS, which are enormous organizations that can raise and spend an unlimited amount of money supporting a particular political candidate as long as they pinky-swear they won't coordinate with the official campaign itself.

They can buy countless ads, send out mailers, hire phone staff, and whatever else they want to push voters one way or the other. They don't have to disclose who their donors are, or how much they contribute.

And evidently the only way to combat a Super PAC is with another Super PAC.

Funny, now we break campaign funding records every fucking election. Look at how impactful billionaire bullshit is at swinging elections! They can donate their morning's income to a candidate and abruptly tilt the scales. The flood of money flowing into ads and travel and paraphernalia and staff and everything else needed to back a candidate is *staggering*.

Democrats have brought some resistance against this policy, but they also claim to have no choice but to fight fire with fire and use Super PACS themselves. Not that it has done them a ton of good when combating textbook fascists.

Once again, it's Conservatives cheering for the most idiotic and corrupt shit, while Progressives helplessly watch their voices get drowned by a torrent of status quo cash.

✻ HOW WE COULD FIX IT ✻

If we can't get the Supreme Court ruling overturned, then we have to legislate this corruption away.

We could amend the Constitution to undeniably state that money is not speech and corporations are not people.

We could implement regulations that limit campaign spending.

We could require these Super PACS and similar groups to disclose all donors and the amount given.

We could require transparency on all advertisements, both physical and digital, as to who really paid for the ad.

And we could require that politicians wear patches with the company logos of their highest donors, racer-style. Only sort of joking.

Do politicians on either side of the aisle actually *want* to stop the flow of billions of dollars into their campaigns? Do any of them actually give a shit what we the people want, or just what the wealthy want? Exactly.

AGE AND TERM LIMITS

One of the biggest reasons we are in this mess is the marked absence of a proverbial asteroid hitting the White House. We need a political extinction-level event to remove the fucking dinosaurs in charge.

We've got geriatrics with one barely functional foot in the grave making landmark decisions, terminally ill elderly given command of critical committees, and dementia-laden leaders of the free world.

If they were out here planting trees for a better, brighter future and the benefit of our children that'd be fine, I suppose. But instead they just plant the annuals that get them elected and then abandon them to starve and wither in the garden.

These people work far past the normal retirement age and cling to their power until their last gasp. It's embarrassing.

"Well just vote them out!" Except it's not always that easy to primary a sitting Congressperson.

It needs a shit load of money to garner local support, and more importantly it requires the support of the political party itself. You have to navigate all the backstabbing, gatekeeping, seniority, fundraising, and other bullshit political games to have a chance against the Old Guard.

Think about how out of touch your average Boomer can be. Now imagine they are career politicians.

They are comfortably wealthy. They've had socialized medicine for most of their working life. They have superb compensation benefits. They are always on vacation. They don't even have to come in for every vote. They allocate most of their work to younger aides.

There are layers and layers of being out of touch with everyday voters. The older they get, the fewer shits they seem to give.

I don't want to devalue the experience that comes with age, but there needs to be a line drawn. And younger leadership is evidently the only way we will get actual progress in this country.

⚒ HOW WE COULD FIX IT ⚒

I don't know the best numbers. The Congressional age limit should be retirement age at least, though I'd prefer younger still.

Term limits could be set as a maximum number of *terms* — say 4–6 — or as a maximum number of *years*, like 12–18.

Include the Supreme Court in this too. A lifetime appointment is indefensible given how outrageously political that "independent" body has become. I rant more on them in the Justice section.

CLOSING RANT

In my home state of Texas (groan), Republicans are always campaigning on how everything would go to shit if the state was ever again lead by those dirty Democrats.

Despite being the second largest economy in the country, our infrastructure ranks in the middle, our median household income ranks in middle, our unemployment ranks in the middle, our education ranks near the bottom, our health outcomes rank near the bottom, our incarceration rate ranks near the top, and our uninsured rate is dead last.

Republicans have had a majority or total control over this state for nearly *30* miserable years, and every meaningful quality of life metric for regular, working-class families has declined — healthcare, housing, public education, infrastructure, wages, and more. Maybe that's why Cancun looks so nice to our Senator Rafael.

You mean to tell me that the second largest economy in the country can't set itself to a higher standard in all these categories?

Republicans aren't even capable of making a wealthy state like Texas great, so why would anyone trust them with the whole nation!?

It doesn't matter. Nothing will change until we radically restructure our voting systems — from infrastructure and access, to the physical ballots.

Otherwise we're eternally stuck between the party of stupidity and evil and the party of meager progress and constant compromise.

DONALD J. TRUMP

IN TRUMP
WE TRUST

DONALD J. TRUMP

This is your guy, Conservatives? This is *really* your fucking guy?

Conservatives that rage about the influence of the wealthy and the "coastal elite" — This is your guy?

A guy born with a bejeweled spoon in his mouth, living in a gaudy golden tower and a seaside palace. A guy representing the poster child of unearned privilege, meritless success, and sickening avarice. A guy obsessed with being included among the Hollywood stars and brushing shoulders with the aristocracy. A true coastal elite without an ounce of hard, honest work to justify it. This is your guy?

Conservatives that would revere a one-religion Christian America and idealize "traditional family values" — This is your guy?

A guy infamous for paying hush money to a porn star for sex after his third wife birthed his fourth kid. A guy tear-gassing peaceful protesters to hold a Bible upside down in front of a church for the camera. A guy that craves worship, values money over everything, and spews hate and lies with every breath. A walking personification of the Deadly Sin's extremes. This is your guy?

Conservatives that are so concerned with the safety of our children and the specter of the pedophilic elite — This is your guy?

A guy recorded bragging about interrupting pageant girls while they change clothes, and about his fame-given power to grab their privates. A guy who has publicly joked about dating his young daughter and has repeatedly minimized or dismissed serious allegations of abuse in others. A guy frequently photographed and filmed with the infamous Jeffrey Epstein, who socialized with him and openly spoke of their friendship, and who offered well-wishes to Ghislaine Maxwell after her arrest. A cesspool of disturbing rumors, sexual allegations, and deeply questionable relationships. This is your guy?

Conservatives that see successful business leaders as the best and brightest among us — This is your guy?

A guy notorious for a string of bankruptcies, bailouts, lawsuits, and fraudulent schemes. A guy revealed as so unreliable and debt-laden that multiple banks reportedly refused to work with him. A guy whose signature book on making deals and good business was penned by a ghostwriter. An inept fool that would've been better off parking his undeserved inheritance in an index and leaving it there if he hadn't milked the once-noble presidency. This is your guy?

Conservatives that subscribe to the cringeworthy "Alpha Male" perspectives about strength, intelligence, and peak male attraction — This is your guy?

A guy allegedly wearing lifts, painting his face orange, and boasting official medical reports on height and weight so improbable they spark widespread mockery and disbelief. A guy long rumored to have paid for more companionship than he ever earned with charm or wit. A guy recurrently accused of cheating at sports and famously mocked for his stupidity by critics and former insiders alike. An unfit, whining, phony, incompetent manchild. This is your guy?

Conservatives that place incalculable value on respect for the military and honoring our veterans — This is your guy?

A guy with scores of documented instances of disrespecting both active and veteran service members. A guy openly believing that veterans get PTSD because they are "not strong." A guy mocking POWs by saying they aren't heroes for getting caught. A draft-dodging, war criminal-pardoning, military parade-forcing traitor. This is your guy?

Conservatives that fret about the influence of a shadow government, foreign influence, and political corruption — This is your guy?

A guy so mired in ethical scandals he has everyone researching emoluments clauses and bribery laws. A guy cozying up to oligarchs, authoritarian regimes, and foreign adversaries so frequently that even their state-run media praises the influence they have over him. A guy appointing some of the wealthiest and least qualified Cabinets in modern history and granting an unelected foreign billionaire unfettered access to our government systems. A living invitation to daylight conspiracies, an unsettling advantage to rival powers, and a figure seen by many as a deeply compromised asset. This is your guy?

A lying, cheating, grifting, scandal-soaked, ego-driven, trust-fund billionaire, and wannabe king — *This is your fucking guy?*

Man, I don't think anyone embodies this country's political, moral, and human failures so well. Such a disgraceful, corrupt, hopeless moron elevated by Conservatives to one of the most powerful positions in the world. America's best, apparently.

It really *should* be surprising how he came to be president twice. It should. But anyone paying attention knows how we got here. Trump *is* the Republican party.

Look at how they all tuck their tails between their legs and let him topple over the country, even after he attacks their character, demeans their families, and threatens their careers! They are all complicit. And every single Trump voter shares the responsibility.

I am completely baffled by the count of suckers he manages to surround himself with at all times. Never mind that towering landfill of discarded loyalists behind him! *You* are Trump's super special sycophant and will be totally safe from his ire.

Nah, *we're* the ones with "Trump Derangement Syndrome".

Nothing else illustrates the premise of this obnoxious book better than the notion that a man like Donald John Trump could be their chosen candidate three fucking times.

These people really looked at Clinton, Biden, and Kamala and saw something worse than that man? Ah but then we get into the Republicans that "didn't vote for Trump, just voted for the *platform*."

Oh okay, okay. So all those personal attacks against every Democrat you hate, all the judgment and venom towards past Democratic presidents and nominees — that was because the person holding the office is meaningless to you? I see. Yes, very fair coverage.

Those people like my dad didn't vote for *Trump*! They just voted for Republicans! They can't be blamed for all the damage he causes, right? The leader of the government has nothing to do with the platform of a party at all — unless it's a Democrat of course.

The wanton corruption, the erosion of our soft power, the severing of our longest alliances, and the enrichment of our worst enemies is all *Trump* stuff that they didn't vote for! *wink*

At the end of it all, Trump is just a puppet for the Conservative elitist think tanks. He's a figurehead for Republican policy goals. He's a useful idiot for foreign adversaries.

STUPID, EVIL, OR BOTH

Trump *is* stupidity and evil personified in a final cancerous form, but he is, perhaps fortunately, too stupid to come up with nightmares like Project 2025 himself. Aside from being a serial liar, that's why Trump so habitually "never heard of that" or "knows nothing about that". It's his favorite excuse in those rare times a reporter asks real questions.

This gets said often, but if Biden or Obama did a miniscule fraction of the kind of crap Trump and his cronies pull off — or even just *said* a microscopic sliver of the same unhinged, authoritarian nonsense — Republicans would collapse in droves of heart palpitations and Olympic-level pearl-clutching.

Nothing highlights the utter, irredeemable hypocrisy of all Republicans more than the existence of the Trump presidencies. It perfectly encapsulates the total vaporization of their credibility, their morality, their ethics, and any crumb of respect I could ever have for them.

The Republicans in Congress have always possessed the power to stop everything Trump is doing, restore the rule of law, and defend the Constitution. They have had the power this whole time. They don't use it because they simply don't want to. They saw his first term and collectively decided they were okay with bringing a twice-impeached felon back to the helm of the White House.

Trump is *exhausting*. Truly fucking exhausting.

The constant deluge of scandals, the ferocious avalanche of constitutional crises, the maddening barrage of hypocrisies, the vast mycelium of lies, the grand mountain of unpunished betrayals, the swift erosion of justice, the creeping threat of full-blown fascism…it's exhausting and heartbreaking.

Yet his supporters everywhere watch with glee as centuries of diplomacy are shattered and trillions of dollars are shredded to appease the ego of a petty, crooked, self-obsessed demagogue.

And it's Conservatives driving it all — both the repugnant Republican enablers and the docile Democrats that reach across the aisle for a place in an authoritarian regime.

🛠 HOW WE COULD FIX IT 🛠

Shit, that's like asking for the cure to cancer. And Trumpism *is* a cancer.

But there really is plenty that could be done to prevent or at least diminish the chances of another Trump.

We would have to begin with getting rid of the first-past-the-post system and replace it with some version of ranked or rated choice voting (which I talked about previously).

We'd need to enact sweeping, radically aggressive anti-corruption legislation and establish an effective, formidable ethics committee.

We'd need to end Citizens United (and therefore Super PACS), write stronger anti-bribery clauses, impose clearer rules on official communication (like posting to your followers about what fucking stocks to buy), and, most critically, heavily boost the enforcement of, and penalties for, breaking these rules.

Oh and maybe don't allow convicted felons and impeached officials to run for office?

THE HYPOCRISY BONUS ROUND

The game is called "Imagine if any Democratic leader had ______________________"!

So, how would Trumpers, Republicans, and Conservatives alike react if a Democrat had:

-   Deliberately withheld disaster relief from Republican-led states as political retribution.

-   Orchestrated the roundup of individuals for deportation without due process and theatrically shipped them to foreign, infamously horrific prisons.

-   Nominated and defended someone accused of child exploitation to serve as the Attorney General.

-   A childishly immature history of late-night, confused, incoherent, all-caps rants on social media.

-   Let an unelected billionaire and a gaggle of inexperienced cronies dig through government data and various systems free from standard oversight.

-   Directed government business toward their personal companies, enriching themselves by billions while in office.

-   Justified in earnest the idea of running for an illegal third term.

-   Ordered public schools to discriminate specifically against right-wing viewpoints and students.

-   Happily accepted millions of dollars in payments from business figures allegedly seeking favorable treatment or protection from economic policy changes.

-   Nominated their own children and other family members as senior White House advisors despite them lacking relevant government experience.

- Transformed the White House lawn into an advertisement for a top campaign supporter's business.

- Raked in gifts worth hundreds of millions of dollars from foreign governments, even those widely known for ties to past terrorist attacks against the U.S.

- Utilized the police to raid the headquarters of an independent peace organization.

- Maintained a personal and social connection with people convicted of sex trafficking minors.

- Prohibited certain terms and concepts deemed unfavorable to left-wing ideology from appearing in official government communications and websites.

- Vaunted on record about using their fame and power to sexually assault pageant girls.

- Elicited hundreds of lawsuits for unpaid debts, discriminatory practices, and alleged fraud.

- Released a smartphone line with their own branding and managed by their own business while in office.

- Yapped comments widely criticized to be inappropriate and suggestive about young girls, including references to their own adolescent children.

- Overseen the gassing of peaceful right-wing protesters just to stage a photo-op and hold a Bible upside down.

- Brushed off their Secretary of Defense repeatedly using unsecured communication mediums for extremely sensitive military operations.

- Vilified ring-wing news outlets by constantly calling them fake and liars.

- Instructed the Department of Justice to fire every attorney appointed by the previous Republican administration.

- Organized a wasteful military parade to celebrate their own birthday like a dictator.

- Used a visit to Arlington Cemetery to film a campaign ad and berated a service member who asked them to stop.

- Spent hundreds of millions of taxpayer dollars to play more golf than many previous leaders combined.

- Leveraged and advertised their own publicly traded stock with their own name as the ticker symbol.

- Yelled dubious claims about their personal physical health test results, including metrics as easily recognizable and verifiable as height and weight.

- Required government staff and visiting officials to stay in hotels and properties they personally owned.

- Altered an official hurricane forecast map for a political stunt.

- Pushed multiple crypto memecoins days before inauguration, raked in hundreds of millions dollars, then hosted an exclusive dinner to thank the top investors.

DONALD J. TRUMP

- Engaged in a stock trading controversy widely described as one of the most blatant insider trading schemes in political history.

- Deployed the National Guard to suppress a largely peaceful right-wing protest, then threatened that state's Republican governor with arrest.

- Claimed they owned the tallest building in the city right after terrorists destroyed the Twin Towers.

- Hired a foreign anti-democracy billionaire to create a comprehensive database of every U.S. citizen.

- Impudently defied court orders multiple times, including those from the Supreme Court.

- Lambasted prisoners of war as losers despite themselves avoiding military service through multiple deferments.

- Delayed transparency with their tax returns to the point of effectively refusing to release them.

- Referred to a deadly pandemic as a "Red state issue" and pledged to deny aid to states governed by political opponents.

- Extorted a foreign leader by withholding Congressionally approved funds while seeking dirt on a political rival.

- Nabbed dozens of boxes containing sensitive government documents and stored them at a private residence, prompting federal investigations.

- Welcomed the plan of imposing martial law over a fabricated national emergency.

- Implemented a massive government loan program for businesses, stripped oversight, and enabled rampant fraud.

- Threatened to invade neighboring countries and other sovereign nations just to claim resources.

- History with infidelity, betrayal, and abuse towards their spouses.

- Jeered at a disabled reporter right in front of a large audience.

- Established a new federal department dedicated solely to protecting the values of a single non-Christian religion.

- Forbade Fox News, OANN, Newsmax, or other Conservative news outlets from access to the White House press pool.

- Fired the Joint Chiefs of Staff of the military to replace them with personal political loyalists.

- Relentlessly abused pardon powers to free white-collar criminals and reward political allies for loyalty and their willingness to obstruct justice.

- Enjoyed frequent praise from foreign state-run networks for advancing the interests of adversarial regimes.

- Yearned for absolute authority while glorifying some of the cruelest dictatorships and our longest-standing enemies.

- Earned dozens of felony convictions for financial crimes.

- Promised to operate the country like one of their numerous bankrupted business ventures.

- Suspended the enforcement of anti-bribery laws and dismantled key government ethics oversight committees.

- Thousands of documented false or misleading statements during their first term alone, according to fact-checking groups.

- Employed campaign funds as hush money in connection to an extramarital affair with an adult film actress.

- Intensively refused to accept the outcome of an election they lost, and purportedly orchestrated a fake electors scheme to nullify the results.

- Nudged their base at a rally, urging them to fight those election results, leading directly to a violent insurrection — then pardoned those involved, including those that assaulted police officers — then removed federal investigators assigned to the insurrection case — then pushed public schools to rewrite history and teach that the election was stolen.

Now imagine a Democrat leader did *all* of this, not just one of these things (I purposefully flipped some colors and parties around to make the point).

I just threw this list together from memory while sitting on the couch next to my partner. And the likelihood that people will read all that and notice many, many forgotten transgressions is pretty fucking telling.

Conservatives would have no standards without double standards.

CAPITALISM

CAPITALISM

Anyone who thinks we're not steadily sliding into some corpo-theocratic-oligarchal dystopia is either deeply privileged or willfully blind to the obvious.

The problem isn't capitalism itself…not exactly. It's not the fundamentals of competition, innovation, and a market that can freely react to all the various economic factors in play. That's not the problem.

The problem is this *illusion* that the market has ever been truly "free" from the beginning, or that everyone has an equal chance.

The problem is a purposeful lack of punitive enforcement for financial crimes and the weakening of guardrails against corruption.

The problem is that many humans are selfish, ruthless, and willing to exploit others no matter the cost, and capitalism *greatly* rewards this sociopathic behavior.

The problem is *unregulated* capitalism spreading its ill effects like wildfire consuming a forest. It's a system that places more value on freeing and enabling a handful of arsonist billionaires than eliminating the enslavement and suffering of the workers whose toil grew the trees.

It's funny, in a facepalm sort of way, debating with Conservatives about the current state of our economic systems.

They'll agree that wealth inequality is a deepening concern. But then they'll uplift the Congressional millionaires keeping minimum wage and poverty synonymous.

They'll agree that the foundation is broken to some degree. But then they'll chant in support of deregulation and union-busting.

They will agree with Progressives about how the elite are out of control. But "their" ultra-wealthy are fine.

Conservatives have so much faith that a system will magically heal itself despite that system consistently and quite tangibly crumbling in multiple ways. The rest of us can clearly see that the cancer is metastasizing.

It's worse than that frog in boiling water metaphor because Conservatives can feel the scalding bubbles around them. It hurts! And they still defend the stove.

FEDERAL MINIMUM WAGE

This concept was originally established under New Deal Democrats back in 1938 to combat the Great Depression (also caused by unregulated capitalism). It was a generally fair and livable income meant to serve as a safety net for workers and bolster a struggling economy.

Nowadays, in our modern capitalistic society, minimum wage can be accurately interpreted as, "If I could legally pay you less, I would. You are worth the absolute minimum financial input from me, regardless of how much value you bring me. Fuck you."

It's bumped up 22 times since 1938. Nearly every time it was a Democrat president pushing for it or a Democrat-controlled Congress passing it. And nearly every time it was the Republicans opposing increases, with only the more moderate among them showing support.

The Conservatives have only gotten worse in their staunch opposition to increasing these poverty wages. As of writing, the federal minimum wage sits at $7.25/hour and has not budged since 2009.

Two thousand fucking nine. It is 2025.

I don't know if any of you red-hats have seen prices lately, but $7.25/hour is basically unlivable in this country.

There are countless analyses out there giving the breakdown of just how unlivable and unsustainable $7.25/hour is, how a sharp increase would not collapse the world economy, how the cost of both living and education went on an exponential path upwards while wages have been on a limp linear path, etc. etc.

This book only has one chart so, if your blood pressure sits at a healthy spot, I encourage you to look at some of those breakdowns and give your vessels a workout.

Why the fuck are Conservatives so determined to keep wages stagnant while the "elite" they claim to despise get wealthier and wealthier? I thought you guys hated the elite class?

So let me rant about the things I've heard them say in regard to increasing the federal minimum wage. I conveniently ordered them from what I consider to be least misguided to the most!

- They argue that a federal minimum wage ignores the regional cost of living differences

Regional differences assuredly exist, and $25/hour in Podunk, Arkansas is going to have a much more significant impact than $25/hour in New York or whatever big city.

The fact is that $7.25/hour is shit pay pretty much anywhere in the country and a raise needs to happen anyway. I'm totally fine with regional differences being looked at, but we're talking about the *baseline* livable wage for people.

Additionally, there are *far* more people living in urban areas than Podunk, Arkansas. Why is national progressive policy always so tightly hamstrung by the needs of the few?

Well because Conservatives think that land can vote, but that topic is a couple sections back.

This is still a valid point for regional phase-in strategies, and it is definitely worth keeping in mind when setting a new number.

However this argument, as with all of them, is no reason to sit and do nothing about the laughably low minimum wage.

Plenty of states have already ignored the Fed and have set their own state minimum wages, which is wonderful! But many other states, predominantly Red ones, look at the Fed rate and match it because why would they go any higher when they don't have to?

- They are worried about job losses and the health of small businesses or low-margin companies

If your business — however small or low-margin or whatever — cannot exist unless you pay your workers as little as legally possible, then your business does not deserve to exist in its current shape with its current strategy. It's really that simple.

The notion that the "free" market will slowly drive those companies out of business for want of labor is true… you know…unless you look at mega-corps paying the minimum. Those get to pay like shit *and* take government subsidies!

Here's a crazy proposal — subsidize small businesses and *stop* subsidizing the largest, most profitable companies! If your product is good or your service is exceptional, people *will* purchase your goods and services even if they are more expensive. *That* is a free market at work.

This is another time when a gradual phase-in strategy could be implemented. Small businesses *would* possibly initially struggle, which is where subsidies could come in. But rewarding big businesses and billionaires for exploiting poverty wages is unethical nonsense.

- They are confident that prices will soar to accommodate higher wages

I've seen numerous analyses on the whole price increases after wage increases thing, with all of them saying that prices would only rise a modest amount, and it'd be primarily limited to industries with the highest labor costs.

I'm sure a handful of you have seen the thing where a burger might go up 1-2% for every 10% jump in wages or something like that.

Yes, a big hike in minimum wage could make costs go up. It should go without saying that the capitalists are going to pass extra costs onto the consumer in some way. Like with tariffs…you fucking morons.

But consumers will also be *able* to spend more. Any marginal price jumps will be heavily outweighed by the growth in disposable income. It's a net positive.

Something else many Conservatives ignore about this point is the productivity side of fair wages.

Productivity has astronomically improved through technology like automation and software efficiencies. Did this huge boost to productivity lead to hugely boosted wages? Of course not. It trickled down from the roof to the C-suite and pooled there.

Additionally, better wages (and generally better worker benefits) lead to employee loyalty. A concept long, long gone in the workforce because companies don't reward it anymore!

If your workers are well-paid, happy, healthy, productive, etc., they will *stay* with you. Turnover will plummet, heavily reducing the overhead on training costs. You will have better-run businesses from experienced, proud managers. The overall quality of your business will fly up, which will likely multiply your net income.

It's a win-win all around, but it requires time and sacrificing short-term profits, which is why Conservatives resist.

The final point I want to make on this is that there are plenty of companies that are known for compensating their workers exceptionally well and are still very successful — Costco, Trader Joes, Buc-ee's, In-N-Out Burger to name only a few.

Conservatives are aware enough to boycott various businesses for political transgressions, so they must know that solid companies that utilize an abundance of "low-skill" laborers (hate that phrase) can be both very profitable *and* pay their employees desirable wages.

- They claim entry-level work for teens will be replaced by working adults

This is such a silly point to me. Do Conservatives realize that the primary reason teens need to work in the first place is because wages are so pitiful that the family unit needs another income source to survive?

Why is that okay? Shouldn't they be focusing on their education, or what they want to study in college, or what trade they want to pursue? Shouldn't teens be enjoying a bit of their youth before the capitalist hope-crushing machine clamps upon their dreams?

I have no objection at all to a motivated highschooler wanting to earn extra money for luxuries, or a passionate kid eager to land a valuable internship somewhere.

I also understand that some kids grow up in a difficult household and their parents can't or won't provide for them, necessitating a job. That's heartbreaking, and I wouldn't want them to be overlooked for employment because of their age.

However, the reality is that roughly 80% of minimum wage jobs are held by adults, most of whom are over 25 years old. It's highly unlikely that raising the federal minimum wage would meaningfully reduce teen employment when adults are already the overwhelming majority of minimum-wage workers.

So Conservatives are telling me they can't raise the minimum wage because otherwise teens might have to…*checks notes*… not work? Do the children actually yearn for the mines? Shouldn't we stop and ask young people what *they* want?

- They insist that wages should be set by a natural economic system and not by the government

This point takes the spot for the weakest argument on this topic for me because the only reason we are in this mess is insufficient federal involvement in the "free" market system.

It's like those hilariously self-owning memes Conservatives like to put online with some disastrous scene in the background — cars on fire, droves of homeless people walking around, raw dystopia stuff — and the caption is like, "This is the future Liberals want!!"

Hello? That's the present! That photo was taken yesterday! In a late-stage capitalist hellscape!

There you have it. These hollow arguments are some of the many reasons why Conservatives feel that you, lowly laborer, deserve to stay impoverished and unappreciated.

We're not even talking about a wage that lets someone *thrive* like the old minimum wage sometimes allowed. We're talking about what's *barely livable* and Conservatives are still against it.

They'll stagnate wages and keep millions of workers one missed paycheck away from homelessness, then they'll outlaw homelessness.

✂ HOW WE COULD FIX IT ✂

If we're not going to do some kind of Universal Basic Income plan, then we need to bring wages far up. Or both.

We should mandate a substantial federal minimum wage increase to something actually decent for once.

We should add subsidies to small businesses that deserve it, with far more oversight than goddamn PPP loans got.

We should eliminate subsidies to large businesses that can easily withstand labor cost adjustments.

We *can* allow states some leeway in determining regional minimum wage phase-in strategies.

Not much else to say other than, "Fucking raise it, assholes."

EXECUTIVE PAY

Now that I've ranted about what the bottom earners make, let's complain about the top earners. It's seriously out of hand.

Back in the 1960s, the CEO-to-worker pay ratio was something like 20:1 and it was all cash and bonuses. In the early 1990s, compensation began shifting to things like stock options and that ratio went up to around 60:1. And in ten short years it flew to nearly 400:1 and hovered.

As of 2025, the estimate for the average CEO-to-worker pay ratio in just the S&P 500 is 285:1. Conservatives are gonna argue about median versus mean and certain outliers making things look skewed… blah blah blah get off your knees. But fine, I'll stick with 285 for the rant.

Now you mean to tell me — with a straight face — that the CEO is doing 285 times the work? "No, but they are taking on all the risk! They deserve that!" Oligarch-jerking nonsense. Wipe yourself off.

These executives could be inconceivably dogshit at their job, as many are, and still get golden parachutes big enough to blot out the sun. The amount of money they get for *sucking* at their job is more money than most Americans would make in dozens of lifetimes. So don't tell me these executives deserve it for whatever microscopic risk they shoulder.

The bulk of their over-inflated compensation comes from stock shares. Apparently over 80% of executive pay is non-salary, which means they don't have to pay income tax rates on it! All they pay is capital gains tax *if* they sell! And by virtue of the various tricks the wealthy employ (Taxes section), they don't ever really *need* to sell to survive.

Even worse, compensation is a tax-deductible line item for businesses, which means they can gift the CEO a dragon's hoard and write it off!

In the end, the executives get more money *and* pay less taxes than their average workers. And those workers, whose labor allows the company to exist and excel, have the pleasure of subsidizing these policies through the aforementioned write-offs.

Even though the workers are more and more productive, generating more and more value for society and these companies alike, their salaries have barely kept up with inflation, if at all. Meanwhile executives can delegate responsibilities to scores of sycophantic VPs and uptight middle managers and then go fuck off playing golf until the next shareholder meeting. Wrote an email — Done for the day! FORE!

Our only reward for hard work is *more* work. We don't get real raises. We don't get job security. We don't get healthcare. We don't get more time off. All we get is to see our boss celebrate a bigger bonus and flaunt new assets while inflation-backed corporate hunger devours our meager "Cost of Living Adjustments".

Yeah dude, inflation is only 2%. Weird how everything in my life costs 30-50% more every other season.

Surely they'll exhaust their supply of excuses for price gouging us eventually, right? Haha, right?

Conservatives will argue that it's the ever-mysterious and all-powerful "free" market that dictates this revolting disparity in compensation. So yeah I guess let's just do nothing about addressing any concerns because the infallible *market* deems it so!

When some cringey billionaire AfD-loving blowhard can somehow "work" as CEO of *multiple* companies while having time to post memes and inflammatory conspiracies all day, maybe the job of CEO isn't as valuable as capitalism claims.

⚒ HOW WE COULD FIX IT ⚒

The Taxes section of this fuming book goes into my rants about fixing some of this inequality through tax code reform. There are lots of suggestions out there for regulating the absurdity of executive pay, but here's how *I* would want things to be for nearly every company.

I'd want to spread the wealth of a company through what would essentially be a huge profit-sharing program.

I'd start by capping executive compensation to some fixed ratio compared to median worker salary — maybe around 40:1 — which *includes* stock and other non-salary compensation.

Then, any excess is shared down the organizational chain. Everybody gets raises, everybody gets stocks, etc. etc. If your company is remarkably successful, congratulations! Your executives still make a ton of money, *and* all of your workers that made it happen are wealthy too!

From the janitor's closet to the C-suite.

Now your company can be rigorously selective about who it hires, ensuring the best quality employees you can and limiting turnover. You can set up a "probationary" period where the stock options or whatever don't come into play until some months after employment.

And since your shareholders are also your employees, there can be votes on what sort of expansion and other projects should be implemented. It would be like replacing the Board of Directors model with a democratic, employee-driven model.

I'm confident there are companies out there that operate exactly like this, and I bet their workers are pretty fucking stoked to be a part of that form of generous, loyalty-rewarding organization.

The government can't *mandate* that a company operates like this, so it comes down to tax reform and altering our perspective on what executives actually deserve.

These are just my ramblings on a solution. There is *something* that can be done to make this less nauseating.

EMPLOYER-BASED INSURANCE

Without a nationalized health system, like most advanced countries have, we Americans are all forced to wade through the private sector swamp for our "benefits".

Oh, but that wasn't quite restrictive enough for Conservatives, so they decided that "affordable" benefits should only be accessible to those that are employed! There's no policy dictating how "good" those benefits have to be or what they should cost, just that the "best" benefits are found through employers because they are footing a chunk of the bill.

During World War II, companies started offering health insurance as a benefit in lieu of increasing wages. Then the IRS said that those employer contributions to health insurance were tax-exempt. So instead of companies simply paying their taxes and the government creating a nationalized healthcare system with those taxes, we subsidize these companies with huge tax breaks and *they* provide our insurance.

Ah but not quite, because it's not like that coverage is free to us as valued employees. We, of course, still have to pay gut-punching premiums and inane deductibles and all that other bullshit. It's the classic privatization double whammy!

Democrats have historically tried to push us towards a single-payer model, while Republicans have fiercely opposed anything but the privatized, employer-sponsored nightmare we have now.

This system leaves people feeling trapped in a job they may hate, lest they go without healthcare.

If you lose your job due to layoffs or an accident or something, you lose your healthcare too.

It neglects anyone without a traditional job, such as gig workers.

It's a more expensive, more convoluted, less efficient, bureaucratic bloat-loaded disaster.

So naturally, Conservatives defend it.

⚒ HOW WE COULD FIX IT ⚒

Read my Healthcare section. Conservatives be warned: I talk about single-payer healthcare *gasp*.

PTO AND FAMILY LEAVE

We are the *only* economically advanced country in the world that does not require employers to provide paid time off, including parental leave.

The European Union mandates a minimum of 20 days of paid vacation annually, with many countries offering additional public holidays and extended leave.

Maternity leave across EU member states averages around 24 weeks, with several countries providing over 30 weeks of paid leave. Paternity leave varies, but all EU countries are required to offer a minimum of 10 days of paid leave.

The U.S. requires nothing. *NOTHING!*

Oh but we have FMLA, right? Sure, but it's unpaid! All it says is that they can't fire you for those times you need off. They don't have to pay you, and there's still restrictions on that!

Ask a Conservative how they feel about all that.

It's *"dirty socialism"* to help keep your workers' mental and physical health in a good place.

It's *"government overreach"* to provide mothers and fathers adequate time with their newborns before getting back to the grind.

It's an attack on the *"free" market* if you try to force companies to provide these benefits for the workers that power the gears of capitalism.

Nice priorities.

Why are Conservatives so masochistic? "Oppress me harder! UwU"

⚒ HOW WE COULD FIX IT ⚒

I say we look at one of the most enviable policies that another country has and try to one-up them! I'm talking 36 fully paid days off a year, additional time for public holidays, 28 weeks of full pay maternity leave, and 14 weeks of full pay paternity leave.

Make it freakishly attractive to work in this country!

I don't know the best numbers out there, but I sure as shit know *zero* ain't right. It's insulting, stupid, and evil.

Pay for it by taxing the rich! Done.

WORKERS UNIONS

You can really see a company's true colors by the way they treat workers who try to unionize. Some companies are willing to spend multiple times more on tools to *fight* unionization than they would spend just making their workers' lives better.

There's a well-funded industry dedicated to providing union-busting services. You'll regularly find these efforts bankrolled by Conservatives like those in the Heritage Foundation. It's always Republicans, y'all.

Do Conservatives realize how much unions have done to improve the average worker's life?

Unions started the overtime pay standard that so many laborers enjoy.

Unions helped to establish the original minimum wage.

Unions fought for FMLA leave.

Unions shaped the anti-discrimination laws in the workplace.

Unions advocated safety regulations like OSHA to protect lives.

Unions gave us the 8-hour workday and a 40-hour week (it used to be worse, mind you)

And that's just the sorts of things they did for *everyone*, including non-union workers.

Members of a strong workers union also get compensation bargaining power, guaranteed PTO, parental leave, pensions, protection from being fired without just cause, and more.

So is it any wonder that corporate-backed Conservative think tanks pour millions and millions of dollars into warring against workers unions?

They employ a host of sleazy tactics to cause union votes to fail.

They'll mandate anti-union fearmongering meetings during work hours.

They'll install cameras and other equipment to monitor for union talks.

They'll hire undercover operatives to sus out union-friendly employees.

They'll schedule intimidation chats with prospective members.

They'll hire armadas of anti-union consultants and lawyers.

They'll outright fire union organizers without just cause.

They do all this nefarious scheming just to avoid the laborers being treated fairly.

It's reprehensible, of course, but it should also be eye-opening to the workers that watch their leadership pulling this shit.

These businesses are so terrified of losing command of their wage-slaves, and they will pay any price but yours to stop it.

✖ HOW WE COULD FIX IT ✖

We need to make it easier to form and join unions, while allowing workers to opt-out if they don't want to pay the dues.

We could also empower sector-specific unions that protect all workers in a given field, rather than the union of a specific company.

We need transparency and accountability for these unions too so that elections, finances, and negotiations are kept honest.

Most of all, though, I want to financially crush any company leaders that dare to be union-busters. Make it illegal to deploy any of those skeezy anti-union tactics and open channels for exposing such activity.

CONSUMER PROTECTIONS AND REGULATION

I know I personally love it when deregulated banks dole out predatory loans and cause a monumental housing crisis.

Or when a drug company uses regulatory capture and an army of lobbyists to market a pain med as non-addictive, causing a widespread opioid epidemic.

Or when a car company tries to cheat emissions tests and pollutes far more than tolerated.

Or when an internet service provider is given subsidies and the freedom to monopolize the industry and impose hidden fees, throttling, and other tactics to save money at the expense of the consumer.

Or when a company poisons and kills hundreds of thousands of vulnerable babies with their marketing tactics for formula.

There are countless cases like these with countless different companies.

Capitalism and cheating, harming, or outright killing the consumers for the sake of profits — two peas in a pod.

Hey, guess which political ideology has a long history of calling for deregulation and dismantling consumer protection law?

Republicans used at least pretend to care about this stuff as much as Democrats. You know…like over a hundred years ago.

It wasn't always so controversial that companies need to be held accountable for wrongdoing, that financial institutions need safeguards in place to protect from market collapse, that our food, air, and water needed to be clean and safe, and that capitalism needed to be regulated to achieve an actually healthy market.

Only in the past several decades have Conservatives decided that protecting the "free" market is more imperative than holding our systems to a higher standard.

Now all they want to do is deregulate and privatize every industry they can — healthcare, telecom, national parks, energy, finance, you name it.

Trump and his fascist-flavored fellows have, as of writing this, already begun work on undermining the EPA, dismantling the CFPB, gutting the SEC, weakening the FDA, and commandeering the FTC among other things. All of these organizations serve vital functions in protecting the rights and safety of consumers, and the Republicans cheer on as these agencies are torn apart.

Conservatives have such an ignorantly misplaced faith in their "free" market, despite hundreds of years of proof that their anti-regulation crusade will lead to disaster.

It's like they forget why these regulations and consumer protection laws were put in place to begin with!

Conservative leaders didn't forget though. They just want to appease their oligarch check-writers, confidently immune to their harmful laws.

⚒ HOW WE COULD FIX IT ⚒

I'd want to usher in a golden age of consumer protection law.

We need to reverse all the destruction of the Trump admin and put the authority back into the hands of consumers.

We need to empower all of these consumer protection agencies and hold companies more accountable for transgressions.

We need to go back to busting up monopolies.

We need more robust truth-in-advertising laws, most importantly for industries that have dreadfully limited oversight.

We need net neutrality to protect the freedom of information.

We need right-to-repair legislation for all tech — from farms to phones.

We need more supervision and regulation for financial firms.

We need to eliminate the practice of junk fees in numerous industries.

We need to expand resources for keeping our food and medicine safe.

I know these are all kind of a vague "just fix it" decrees, but I talk more about what I really want to do in the Justice section of this whiny book — plus this chapter is long already.

Check the "Corporate Crime" header for more. Spoiler alert: I want to financially devastate the people responsible for these anti-consumer acts and see them planted firmly behind cold iron bars.

PRIVATE EQUITY HOMEOWNERSHIP

Homes are meant to be lived in. By families. Not sit empty as "investment vehicles".

Our grievously crooked government just laid back and let foreign nationals and avaricious companies scoop up as much housing property as they could without a single moment of forethought. These firms buy up entire neighborhoods then systematically and collectively crank rent and home values to unreachable heights.

Then wealthier individual opportunists get in on the action and start buying up a few properties to rent out at equally inflated prices. Oh, just an extra home or two to help with retirement, right? I'm an iNveStOr!

Well now all we have is unaffordable homes whose value has exploded relative to median income. We have generations of people that are essentially biding time until their parents pass, hoping to squeeze whatever meager equity they can out of a gravestone to afford life or even their first non-rental. Better hope they never took out a second or third mortgage to pay for the soaring cost of existing!

It's foolish, short-sighted, and greedy. A perfect reflection of American values lately.

This is a both-parties failure. Both Democrats and Republicans have been intentionally useless on this crisis. It's clear neither side wants to regulate an industry that surely boosts their portfolios.

Fixing this sort of thing would probably make home prices plummet. Why would the aging dinosaurs that occupy our government want to do that to themselves? I'm sure a handful of them own a rental or two.

So while Republicans openly position to let the all-knowing "free" market decide whether or not anyone poor should ever own a home, the more conservative Democrats do what they do best and offer lip service and no solution of substance.

This means it's an ideological difference, which is obviously a common point in my rants here. It's progressive Liberals versus regressive Conservatives again and again.

This is first and foremost a *regulation* failure and the mere mention of that word sends Conservatives into a panic, desperately hunting for their bottle of blood pressure pills before parroting the Murdochs like it's their job. The industry needs to be *regulated.* *Wilhelm scream*

⚒ HOW WE COULD FIX IT ⚒

Part of the challenge here is all the different layers that need to be peeled back and sanitized individually.

First we should cap the number of single-family homes that can be owned by one entity. We could employ heavy tax penalties for owning more than two or three homes to disincentivize the practice altogether. This could also include vacancy taxes or absentee owner taxes.

If we make it unprofitable, then buying multiple homes is no longer a compelling business option.

But then you'd have to crack down on the unmitigated landfill of shell companies that exist to obfuscate true ownership. There'd be whole beaches of shells that would pop up overnight to "own" the maximum number of homes. These dummy corps and "holding companies" are a huge pain in other areas too, but that's another topic.

Fine, next you impose an outright ban on private equity and/or foreign ownership of American residences. These are people who will never live in these homes and only see assets to hoard.

Forbidding this was an obvious policy from the start. Idiots.

And then you'd have to implement some kind of federal or state-level laws that define who an eligible purchaser is and write policies that bring maximum transparency to ownership and ownership transfers.

And then finally — and this is my favorite one — continuously monitor for violations and fine everybody lying about their asset situation into oblivion. Anyone caught trying skirt around these rules should be financially ruined.

Make these people afraid to even *attempt* to use family homes as investment vehicles.

UTILITIES

Why did we ever allow private companies to come in and privatize things as crucial as power or water? It just seems mind-boggling that we didn't use imminent domain or something long ago.

Now even the internet is as ubiquitous and essential to our everyday lives as any other public utility. And of course it's Conservatives blocking consumer-friendly legislation there too, like Net Neutrality.

It's all a history of Conservative deregulation and far, far too much confidence in the spirit of a "free" market. As usual.

Corporations care about two things only: short-term profit and long-term profit. And when the government carelessly lets monopolies infect vital industries like utilities, then everyone suffers.

Conservatives will cut funding to public services to intentionally blunt their effectiveness, then shout from the hilltops how much better privatization will be.

Please, let the wealthy businessmen that pay me come in and manage your utilities and it will be so much cheaper and better! Never mind that there's so few, if any, other options where you live! We promise the company has your best interest at heart!

Decades and decades of this mentality have led to some pretty disastrous situations across the country — from dangerously outdated infrastructure to callous price gouging tactics.

These companies answer to no one but investors. They cut corners on maintenance, they raise their rates at will, they abandon rural or low-income areas, and then they take all those profits and lobby Congress to keep their scheme rolling.

They even get billions and billions of taxpayer dollars in subsidies.

So it appears Conservatives would rather our tax dollars subsidize unreliable, profit-driven private utilities than allow the public to fund these projects and reinvest any excess into the local communities.

✗ HOW WE COULD FIX IT ✗

I don't know, there's probably some convoluted legal reason why this can't change any time soon.

Ideally we could at least look at rural, underserved areas, or places that have only a couple of options and install publicly-funded infrastructure to compete with the private companies.

We've seen success with this kind of venture for internet service. Look at places that offer municipal fiber! It's internet funded by the local taxpayers. It's reliable, very cheap, and is subject to public oversight. This kind of model could be implemented everywhere if not for the inevitable backlash of the ISP lobby machine.

I could also probably rant about toll roads for an hour, but I'll spare you.

Really I'm just pissed that the privatization of utilities ever even became a thing. Dictator me would say fuck you to the current companies and give control of utilities to the local communities. Though maybe that's a little extreme even for me. Calm down, Capitalists.

CREDIT CARD INTEREST AND OVERDRAFT FEES

I threw this section in because Conservatives just voted to roll back Biden-era overdraft fee caps and I thought that was such a shocking and unnecessary middle finger to anyone struggling to make ends meet.

Just outrageously heartless.

Credit card interest rates are jaw-droppingly demented, and it's only like this because of deregulation and a Conservative-backed Supreme Court decision. They said that banks can charge as high an interest rate as their state allows, and states *really* want banks to do business with them, so the floodgates opened.

The banks, without blinking, say that interest rates need to be as high as 30% to "offset risk". They're full of it and just want to siphon money from the poorest people who struggle to afford living and rely on credit lines for both necessities and simple pleasures.

As for overdraft fees, I mean it doesn't get much more hostile to the poor than that policy. Charging someone living paycheck-to-paycheck a contemptible fee because their boss didn't pay them on time (or something) is evil.

People can even get screwed over by the processing time it takes the bank itself to get money into someone's account.

Banks make *billions* of dollars every year from overdraft fees. Really think about how ludicrous that is.

Biden comes in and tries to cap those fees at $8. Okay, it's a start.

Welp, then the MAGAs take over again and allow banks to continue their predatory ways.

The cruelty is the point.

🛠 HOW WE COULD FIX IT 🛠

I sort of unrealistically want to de-privatize the banks and create some kind of non-profit, government-owned institution that offers all the usual financial services like credit cards, loans, etc., but at much more reasonable rates.

Barring radical change like that, we can mandate a cap on credit card interest to something more reasonable, like 10%.

We can require banks to follow interest rate laws in the consumer's state, not just the bank's home state.

We can require banks to be more transparent about the financial impact of credit card interest — with repayment timeline estimates, total cost from interest, and more.

We could tie the interest rate to income and help keep the poorest people out of predatory debt traps.

This is a policy and greed situation, not some kind of "free" market burden the selfless banks are taking on. They make a killing off of maintaining the wealth inequality status quo.

That's what happens when Conservatives deregulate everything.

BILLIONAIRES

The final boss of late-stage capitalism — the treasure-hoarding dragons of real life, guarding their mountain of riches with a covetous, fiery fury.

Metaphors aside, these are not healthy people. They have a sociopathy that many in society — particularly Conservatives — celebrate instead of treating it like the sickness it is.

They are addicts. They are hoarders. And they should not exist.

It's funny hearing Conservatives like my dad talk about billionaires. It really just depends on which party these dragons openly support.

If they are a slightly left-leaning billionaire, then my dad thinks they are criminal scum that ought to be financially ruined and imprisoned.

But if they're actively campaigning for "America's Hitler", then my dad praises them as legendary geniuses deserving of every dime.

Nobody "earns" a billion freaking dollars through back-breaking, society-building labor.

Billionaires are the product of a generation that decided to focus on their own limitless enrichment instead of working to make the future better for their children.

They are walking policy failures built on a foundation of worker exploitation, regulatory capture, tax avoidance schemes, government subsidies, and compound interest.

Most people haven't even taken the time to sit down and comprehend how much money $1 billion is. It's a truly surreal, disturbing pile of wealth. And there are people out there with tens or hundreds of billions.

They'll sometimes wait until their death to put all the treasure into some "charitable" foundation that their family is paid to own and operate.

Instead of doing something meaningful for the here and now, they grasp their Precious to their last selfish breath. And we're all left hoping they somehow raised kids with purer hearts.

Conservatives will say, "It's not like they're just sitting on that much cash! You can't take illiquid assets from them! *REEE!*" and then do nothing or even vote to widen our wealth inequality gap.

And so children die hungry. The sick avoid treatment. Education quality falls. The homeless fill the streets. Infrastructure crumbles. Our lifespan shrinks. The world burns and floods.

All so a few dragons can rest in serenity on their mountain of gold.

They could have done the morally right thing and prevented their status as billionaires altogether by selling their assets and spending the excess on humanitarian aid for the rest of their days.

Every single one of them could have shirked the title of "Billionaire" and embraced a legacy of benevolence and world-altering philanthropy.

But they are not good people. Nobody gets to that unimaginable magnitude of wealth without corroding their integrity.

The corruption in their mind focuses on amassing their riches like it's some kind of aristocratic contest — aiming to be the first trillionaire in a fully-realized capitalist nightmare.

Billionaires are not just "the wealthy" among us. They are the twisted offspring born and raised in the warm, welcoming embrace of Conservative fiscal policy.

🛠 HOW WE COULD FIX IT 🛠

I want to go dragon hunting.

Metaphorically.

Most of the hunting tools are in the Taxes section of this unpalatable book. Read there next for more realistic approaches to making these lizards an endangered species.

If I had full control though? I'd set a hard limit on total wealth. Once you reach a billion dollars in assets, you're done. You win capitalism.

Everything earned in excess of that is either distributed to the workers of companies you manage, taxed at 99%, placed into a publicly-managed humanitarian fund that you and your family can't touch, or some combination of the three. That's it. You still have a *billion* dollars in assets that you can use as you see fit.

You get caught intentionally lying about the existence or value of your assets? Whoops, you just lost the right to that treasure and it'll get redistributed accordingly. Thank you for your contribution to society. Also enjoy prison.

Your company goes belly-up and you lose your billionaire status? Welp, sucks to suck. You probably still have hundreds of millions of dollars left to try to get back to a billion, or you can do what normal people would do and fuck off into the sunset living life on easy mode.

"But then all the rich people will just leave!"

Oh, will they? Fine! They barely contribute anything to uplifting society anyway! And guess what? The "free" market will let others take their place and reap the rewards and potential this country has to offer.

I realize that's some radically anti-capitalist ranting right there.

Somewhere a Conservative with a few grand in their savings account is reading all this and seething.

But we seriously have to do *something* about this, folks.

<u>CLOSING RANT</u>

When someone can work full-time and still need food stamps to survive, that's a comprehensive failure of the economic system.

This country shows no respect for its workers outside of the upper class.

Can't get raises. Can't get sick. Can't take time off. Can't band together. Can't *do* anything but start romanticizing the depressing necessity of "grind culture." I have a side hustle too, and I hate it.

Meanwhile billionaires get to keep freely rigging the game and using our tax dollars to feed their mental illness.

You know…if we had affordable healthcare, if higher education was more accessible, if homelessness wasn't an epidemic, if wages had kept up with reality, if our children were safe in school, if justice wasn't only for the poor, if basic worker's rights weren't an afterthought, if shrinkflation and enshittification weren't so common, if companies were held accountable for wrongdoing, if the wealth inequality wasn't so obvious…

…then maybe people like me would have a harder time ranting about unregulated capitalism's abundant failings.

If only.

TAXES

TAXES

Somewhere along the line, Conservatives simply forgot what taxes are actually for. They go around moaning about how "taxation is theft," and the moment a right-wing politician promises to "lower their tax burden," they climax on the spot.

"Taxes are just the gubment stealing my money!" they'll scream as they drive on the freshly paved public road.

"They just want to put regulations on everything and cost all of us more!" they'll whine while drinking safely from the tap.

"I shouldn't have to pay for some librul Democrat's education!" they'll post using the wonder of technology in their palm.

"The Feds just want to spend money on some Leftist woke shit!" they'll assume as we increase our defense budget and cut education for the umpteenth time in a row.

"The IRS is an illegal institution!" they'll argue as they try to lie on their tax return again.

Taxes are a daylight robber to them. Some radical left federal agent comes and steals from their paycheck every other week. That's it. Conservatives appear to put no additional thought into what sorts of things taxes pay for.

Now I will give them *some* credit when they complain about government waste, and spending money on stupid shit. But we just deeply, deeply disagree on what we consider to *be* stupid shit.

So you have to ask Conservatives what they think is the function of the government. What *should* we be using taxes on?

In short, they'll tell you that government is supposed to protect our individual freedom and property, uphold the Constitution, support the "free" market, and enforce laws. Wonderfully vague, but that's what they believe. Sprinkle in some support for "traditional family values" and that's everything. Anything else the government does is overreaching and wasteful.

With those ideals, you can definitely see why they want to spend so much on "defense", the police, and tax breaks for the wealthy.

The military and police protect us from foreign invaders and domestic criminals, and the wealthy own all the property and control the markets. Ergo all of our tax dollars should go towards supporting those things alone. Conservatives don't think the government should be involved in anything else, really.

They of course don't *vote* for this stupidly limited scope of government, but that's what they *claim* they want.

To Conservatives, the government should *not* fight to make its population happy and healthy. The government should *not* strive to maintain competitive education for its youth. The government should *not* help the elderly with financial security in their final years. The government should *not* get involved when businesses do financial or even physical harm to consumers. The government should *not* protect its natural environment.

That's why they hate paying taxes. They see the left-leaning leaders calling for policies to aid citizens, or to pay for school, or to strengthen social security, or to impose fines and regulations…but none of that falls in line with their fundamental beliefs about the role of government. Thus they see it all as wrong and an affront to their paycheck.

All those things the government "shouldn't be involved with" are usually pretty progressive concerns too — healthcare, education, consumer protections, environmental protection, etc. etc.

Conservatives have no quandary whatsoever with a massively bloated and audit-less defense budget, rural towns with police tanks, enormous tax incentives for the 1%, and shredding hundreds of millions of dollars so Trump can play golf all the goddamn time because *those* tax-expenditures line up with their value system. Apparently.

They are right about one thing though — Our tax system *is* a fucking outrage. But it's not because we spend too much on the Progressive agenda. We spend barely anything on progressive anything!

Our tax system is a joke because our spending priorities are so senselessly backwards.

Our tax system feels like theft because our politicians forgot that they are supposed to work for *the people*, not corporations and oligarchs.

Our tax system is a disaster because the wealthiest people and businesses do not come remotely close to paying their fair share towards the society that allows their existence and builds their golden mountains.

It needs a major revamp, and it is *always* Conservatives pushing back on changing the tax code to benefit everyday Americans.

Nearly every single time they win a majority in the House they decimate the tax burden on the wealthy, pay for a fraction of the lost revenue by sowing chaos and slashing funding for everything useful, and then blame Democrats for the shitshow that follows.

So, this is the section where readers learn how we are going to pay for all the radical-left, progressive plans in this grouchy book.

Do you Conservatives want to travel back to when you think your beautiful America was "great"?

Cool, we can start by building a great tax code.

THE CURRENT INCOME TAX SYSTEM

Too many people have no clue how our current income tax system works. I've heard people in my life — grown-ass adults — talking about *refusing* a raise at work because they saw it would bump them into the next bracket and thought they would pay more taxes and lose money. Thats_not_how_any_of_this_works.gif

I briefly discuss educating people about how the current tax system works in the Education section of this fretful book, if you feel like that flavor of depression.

Though in a way, they are right to be skeptical of the system. This shit is structured to siphon as much money from the poorest Americans while leaving the wealthiest people relatively unscathed.

The bracket stops at 37% for income up to infinity! If you make $610k a year then you would pay the same income tax rate as someone raking in $150 billion a year. An exaggerated example, but that's still technically the truth. Does that sound fair to you?

The brackets are spaced out in such a way that the burden is *massive* on anyone making middle-class money and below. It's a huge share of your actual take-home effective wages because so many people are forced to live paycheck to paycheck. The money snatched from poorer people could have a substantial impact on improving their lives, while the ultra-wealthy wouldn't feel a thing.

The skew is egregious, and guess how we got here?

In the earliest days, the wealthiest people only paid like 7% at the top bracket. Whoops, then the Great Depression happened. Then during World War II, FDR needed money to support the troops and rates were raised to as high as 94% for top earners.

After the war, rates fizzled down to about 70% at the top. Then Ronald freakin' Reagan — aka the likely reason why so much in this country sucks and probably the most damaging president until Trump — came in and took a god-cleaver to the top rate, bringing it down to 28%. Reagan did a lot of other loathsome, wealthy-friendly things too, but I won't get into that. He's your average Conservative's hero, though.

After Reagan, the top rate went up to 31% during Bush Sr. (wow, a teensy weensy bump by a Conservative??), and Clinton raised it again to 39.6%. Then the next Bush came in and dropped it back to 35% (ah, back to form), then Obama brought back the 39.6%, then Trump dropped it to 37%.

My point with all that history is that when America was "great" — when businesses were booming and a lower wage job held by just one parent could pay for a house and school and transportation and healthcare and vacations and all the various luxuries a thriving country could offer — the top marginal income tax rate was between 70-91%.

And because of Conservative fiscal policy and the oligarchal reign over our politicians, it's down to 37%.

Now they scratch their heads and wonder why so much sucks.

⚒ HOW WE COULD FIX IT ⚒

I want to shift, or more like *shove*, the brackets to place far more burden on the wealthiest earners.

We can add more granularity to the brackets with more income ranges and more percentages so that there aren't such mammoth jumps between the lower income divides.

And then when we get to the highest earners the rates do this weird thing where they keep climbing! Up and up and up to something like 70%, or 75%, or hell even 90% for people above like $50 million a year!

I don't know the right numbers for the right brackets. But I definitely know that it doesn't stop at 37%. This wouldn't come close to solving everything, of course. It's just one piece to the all-inclusive overhaul that we needed yesterday.

Additionally, I'd passionately support the Wealth Tax idea that's been floating around the progresso-sphere lately. Any assets over a specified minimum, say $50-100 million, get flat-taxed at 3% (or more). Just right off the top. It's said would be several trillion dollars over a decade.

Personally, I think we could go a little harder on that, but maybe a Wealth Tax combined with radically reforming the tax code would be enough to stymie the festering infection of the hyper-wealthy.

FICA TAXES

For those that don't know, FICA taxes are the payroll taxes that come out of your paychecks each period to cover Social Security and Medicare. They currently account for 7.65% of the income — 6.2% to Social Security, and 1.45% to Medicare.

The latter piece is not capped, and anyone making $200,000 a year ($250,000 a year for joint-file couples) or more pays an additional 0.9% towards Medicare.

However, the Social Security piece *is*, moronically, capped.

That 6.2% towards Social Security is only paid on income up to $176,100. This means that some hedge fund "laborer" making $500,000 a year pays just as much towards Social Security as an engineer or a medical professional making $176,100.

A CEO making tens of millions a year in salary alone pays the same rate towards Social Security as one of their minimum-wage employees.

Conservatives have always opposed removing this cap. You see they would rather just keep raising the retirement age so you have to work until you're one foot in the grave.

Lately they've been preaching to remove Social Security entirely! They fabricate evidence of widespread fraud and spawn doubts about the importance of Social Security in their ill-informed base. "It's another way the government is stealing from you! It's a Ponzi scheme!"

They'd rather privatize it so that the whims of oligarchs and market swings can dictate your finances from beginning to end.

Social Security is a societal safety net. It's in the name. It ensures that when a population ages and retires from the workforce, that they have some form of stable income to support a dignified living in their final years on this blue ball.

You work most of your life, paying into a fund that supplies steady financial protection for your retirement. It offers disability insurance, it helps survivors of deceased workers, and it provides some amount of poverty shielding for the elderly, children, and the disabled.

It is not *meant* to be some stupendously lucrative investment vehicle like a private hedge fund. It is *meant* to be exactly what the name suggests: Security.

Lower-income people are not likely to have a pile of extra money lying around for potentially risky investments. Not everyone is able to work consistently due to health issues or disabilities. Sometimes emergencies empty a savings account. The stock market isn't some beacon of stability and has had numerous crashes and wild swings that have a giant impact on personal savings.

Social Security is intended as a shield against all of those shortcomings.

✖ HOW WE COULD FIX IT ✖

How can we make the FICA tax system better?

For one, Social Security needs some love. It *is* in trouble, but not because of the fraud and waste that Conservatives love to lie about. It's in trouble because — surprise surprise — the wealthy do not pay enough into it. That cap is absurdly low. Just idiotically low.

There are several possible methods of making the wealthy pay more into Social Security. We could just raise that income cap to something more reasonable or remove the cap altogether.

We could also create a "donut hole" where the current cap stays for a while as one goes up in income, but then the tax rate rises as you reach a set threshold and beyond. This ensures that the middle class doesn't take the brunt of the new tax burden, and instead the wealthy do.

The Medicare piece of FICA needs a similar treatment in my opinion. We could create more divides where the surtax continues to grow the higher your income. Funding programs like Medicare-For-All would also likely require the minimum Medicare percentage to increase, which is fine since you are no longer paying private health insurance premiums in that scenario (Healthcare section).

An even more important piece, I believe, to ensuring that the wealthy pay their fair share into these systems is to expand the FICA tax to include *all* types of income — particularly capital gains, dividends, and other investment income streams.

As it stands, it's only payroll income. The wealthy don't usually acquire the bulk of their riches through salary. It's through investments and accounting games. If all that shit was subject to FICA taxes, Social Security would positively be able to afford sustainability, and Medicare could be implemented for the whole country.

Really weird how if you just change a bunch of these tax systems to require the rich to pay their fair share, the vast majority of lives improve.

So weird.

TAX AVOIDANCE LOOPHOLES

There are numerous systems in place that allow the wealthy to avoid paying taxes, or that grant them much lower rates than the normal income rates. The tax code is contorted this way on purpose, of course.

The rich lobbied Congress for these laws, or even wrote the text themselves! Many, if not most, of our politicians pad their portfolios utilizing these same policies and loopholes too. Why would they vote to change it? It is intentionally convoluted to give the wealthy a well-stocked tax avoidance toolbox.

There are far too many to list, but these are the handful that I am immediately aware of and want to change.

Capital Gains Tax

Currently, the long-term (i.e. assets held for over a year) capital gains tax rate is dependent on income.

The bottom income bracket for single filers, below about $48k a year, pays 0% on capital gains. The middle bracket, i.e. $48k – $533k, pays 15%. Any income above that pays 20%.

By the way, all the numbers in this chapter are going to be different depending on when you read this. But as of the time of writing, that's what it looks like for capital gains.

Now remember, ordinary income is taxed *way* higher than that. Why? Well because the wealthy don't usually get much in normal income, at least relative to what they make in investments!

So everyone else working regular jobs and bringing actual value to society is likely paying a higher tax rate than people that can sit on their ass and make more money in two minutes of clicking at their stock account than you will in a lifetime.

In my opinion, this shit just full stop needs to be taxed as normal income, *and* be subject to the new marginal tax rates I discussed above. You can adjust the brackets or create a new capital gains bracket system so that this really only affects the hyper wealthy, but the fact that they get away with paying so little is maddening.

This is just me complaining about the percentages themselves — the wealthy have many more tricks as seen below.

The Step-Up Basis System

The step-up basis system is said to be one of the biggest tax-dodging loopholes around. When you read how it works, I hope you get as infuriated as I am about it.

Imagine that I bought $100,000 worth of some stock. 20 years later I die, and that stock is now worth $1,000,000. In a world that makes sense, my heirs would need to pay capital gains taxes on $900,000 worth of profit.

Nope! Not under our current system! My kids can sell that stock and pocket all the profit completely free from taxes because the cost basis "stepped up" to $1,000,000 instead of the $100,000 I originally bought it for. It's like that $900,000 in profit just ceases to exist for tax purposes.

This bullshit creates these dynastic wealth environments we have where so little is actually earned, merely inherited.

This might get overlooked because the ultra-wealthy typically just hang on to these assets without selling them anyway. They can use these assets as collateral for loans or live off of dividends and interest. They don't *need* to sell it. That issue comes up soon.

Still, guess which party implemented this system, and which party has tried some degree of reform several times?

Biden tried to limit or eliminate this loophole for gains above $1 million, but go figure it didn't pass.

The Lifetime Exemption – Estate and Gift Tax

This is a tax policy often referred to as the "Death Tax", expressly by Conservatives that want to make it sound like the evilest thing imaginable. Meanwhile I'm over here thinking it doesn't go far enough.

The estate tax is essentially saying: "At the time of your death, we will determine the value of your assets and liabilities, and anything valued over the Lifetime Exemption gets taxed at a marginal rate."

Currently the Lifetime Exemption is $13.99 million per person. If your estate is worth $20 million, then roughly $6 million is taxable (for single filers). If you're a married couple, then the exemption doubles to $27.98 million. That $20 million estate wouldn't be taxed at all if you are a married couple.

This tax has a marginal system where the rate increases as the value of the estate increases, and caps out at 40% for values above $1,000,000. Well, it's estate values that *exceed* the Lifetime Exemption figure, remember. So again, if a married couple dies and their estate was worth a whopping $27,000,000, then the heirs pay nothing.

The Lifetime Exemption also looks at the total gifts given over the life of the estate-holders.

This would mean if that estate of mine is worth $20 million, and I gave out gifts worth $5 million during my life, then my tax liability is the summed $25 million (estate value + gifts given) minus the Lifetime Exemption of $13.99 million, for a total of about $11 million (which would get taxed at 40%).

Ah but of course there's a caveat. Each year, you are allowed to give up to $19,000 as a gift *PER PERSON* without it counting against your Lifetime Exemption, and it's again double that for a married couple.

This means that some rich mom and pop can gift $38,000 a year *TO AS MANY PEOPLE AS THEY WANT* until they die and it will not count against their Lifetime Exemption.

In my example, if that $5 million in gifts I gave out was actually spaced out around several people over many years and I never gave more than $19k per person per year (or whatever the limit was that tax year), then now my estate tax liability drops from $11 million to $6 million.

You can probably see how easy it would be for hyper-wealthy people to plan ahead in such a way that they avoid paying any estate taxes at all.

The Lifetime Exemption needs to be sizably reduced — maybe to $2-3 million a person — and the top tax rate needs to go up a noticeable amount. In my opinion it should be similar to the income brackets.

We should also tweak the Gift Tax by reducing the annual exclusion amount or even applying stricter rules to assets like stocks.

Reform like this wouldn't be hurting the middle or lower class. Conservative leadership loves to fearmonger their poorer base over this.

It's freaking $14 *MILLION* dollars and double that for a couple!

Yet they successfully convince some impoverished, Red state voter that the Liberals are after their house that's worth $500k or something.

STUPID, EVIL, OR BOTH

Trusts

For when the Lifetime Exemption loopholes aren't good enough, you have trusts! There's GRATS and ILITS and IDGTs and Dynasty Trusts and SLATS and even family-owned LLCs!

I won't get into all of these individually, but it's worth chugging some blood pressure meds and having a read.

They are all various mechanisms that the wealthy use to bypass the Lifetime Exemption and immensely reduce their tax liability. There is a truly labyrinthian mess of accounting tricks at play here allowing the wealthy to hide their riches from taxation, and it's all perfectly legal.

It's by design.

We could do things like limit trust durations, apply capital gains tax to assets shifted to trusts, and remove the various taxable value discounts that these systems use to evade contributing to society.

Carried Interest

This is when some private equity firm or venture fund administrator receives income from the "work" they do managing investments.

They, for some asinine reason, only pay capitals gains tax rates, which I've mentioned are stupidly low. It is essentially their salary, but not being taxed at the 37% rate that normal income would require (or far higher under a reformed system). It needs to be taxed as normal income.

It's worth mentioning that this is more of a symbolic reform rather than one generating a ton of extra tax revenue. It's another towering middle finger to everyone working useful jobs — those keeping the country functioning and productive — that the folks managing the money of the hyper-wealthy don't have to pay normal income tax for their "work".

Pass-Through

Pass-through incentives are a tool that the wealthiest people can use to treat their income as "business income" through LLCs, partnerships, and S corps. They aren't subject to corporate taxes and instead only pay individual income taxes.

Many high-earning professionals use this to pay less than everyone else, because they felt they were getting taxed twice — both a corporate tax and an individual income tax. Why they felt that forming a business should mean they don't have to pay the associated business taxes is beyond me.

The tax avoidance was made far worse when Conservatives implemented their pro-corporate tax bill in 2017 which reduced Qualified Business Income (QBI) by an additional 20%. So in practice, any high-income earner that could easily restructure or reclassify their income as "business profit" got a huge tax cut.

Pretend your LLC made $1,000,000 in profit. Before 2017, that entire amount would have been taxed as ordinary income at your marginal rate. Now, eligible pass-through owners can deduct up to 20% of their qualified business income. So that taxable million could drop to $800k.

It's advertised as being a huge boon to small business owners, and it absolutely is! But the wealthy twist the intent and exploit this system to further slash their societal dues.

There are numerous different reforms that can be implemented to keep the small business aid there, while removing the benefit for wealthy professionals, passive investors, and big businesses.

We could lower the QBI deduction income cap. We could expand exclusions for specific professions and businesses. We could monitor for shell company shenanigans. We can place limits on business size such as net worth, revenue, or employee head count. All sorts of things!

Of course, the 2017 tax changes were structured in ways that disproportionately benefited wealthy individuals and their big businesses, rather than focusing solely on aiding genuine small ones.

Securities-based Lending

This isn't a tax code loophole, per say, but it's absolutely a way that the ultra-wealthy get around having to trigger taxable events when they want to buy their third yacht.

Securities-based lending allows fantastically rich people to offer up assets as collateral for very low interest loans — like rates that us poorer folk never get access to for the loans we need.

They stake public stocks, private stocks, bonds, their second mansion, their luxury car collection, their "fine" art, crypto, and even life insurance policies as collateral for the liquidity these special loans provide. They never have to sell any of this unless they get margin called, and the value of these assets rarely drops far enough for it to change anything.

Bottom line is, they get to keep all their wealth-building assets, they get unfair interest rates for the cash to buy more wealth-building assets, and they never pay a dime in taxes during the process.

You see "loans" are not considered income to be taxed. They can just keep accumulating and accumulating like a low-risk revolving credit line where they also get to deduct the interest from their taxes!

There've been talks about ways to tackle this, but the oligarchal pushback would be that of a dragon's fury.

If it were up to me, I'd want to tax unrealized capital gains of certain limits either annually or at least at the time of death so that they can't just sit on these massive hoards for generations.

We could also cap the interest deduction for these loans so the wealthy can't write that off. My student loans were fucking 6.5% interest btw.

✖ HOW WE COULD FIX IT ✖

If you read it all, you got an idea of how I would want to close these loopholes, but here's a summary:

Significantly raise the capital gains tax rate or create a new marginal bracket system similar to income that spares the lower and middle class and targets the wealthiest investors.

Either eliminate the step-up basis system or set a minimum that taxes everything above something like $1,000,000.

Drastically reduce the Lifetime Exemption value — maybe to around $2-3 million per person. Also bring down the Gift Tax annual exclusion and/or apply stricter rules to certain gifts like stocks.

Close as many loopholes as possible in the trusts space, including tweaks to duration limits, applying capital gains taxes, and removing taxable value discounts.

Treat carried interest as normal income.

Reform the pass-through system in a way that protects small businesses and removes the benefit for the wealthy by lowering the Qualified Business Income cap, expanding exclusions for specific professions and businesses, improving our capacity to monitor for shell company bullshit, and placing limits based on business size metrics.

And finally, implement as many tax policies as you can to make securities-based lending a less lucrative and available option for the affluent to consistently accumulate wealth.

Taxing unrealized capital gains and limiting the interest deduction for SBL would be a start.

Conservatives always lose their minds over reforms like these.

Let me rescue you from the right-wing media spin cycle for a moment: If you were unaware of most of these loopholes or didn't know how they work, chances are their closure wouldn't affect you in the slightest.

You can stop bootlicking the wealthy. They don't care about you.

OFFSHORE TAX HAVENS

While we're on the topic of tax loopholes, let's talk about the Cayman Islands, Bermuda, Panama, the Bahamas, and other places that reportedly house something like 10% of the *entire* world's wealth.

Here's a radical opinion: Businesses operating in this country should be taxed *in this country*! Profits made in this country should be taxed *in this country*! Businesses should not get special tax benefits just for existing!

The accounting gymnastics that corporations use to avoid paying their fair share of taxes in this country, and the Conservative tax codes that allow or endorse the behavior, have robbed us of *TRILLIONS* of dollars over the years.

TRILLIONS of dollars — hundreds of billions every year — that could have gone towards healthcare, infrastructure, education, green initiatives, or any other thing this country so desperately needs.

They'll shift profit centers to low-tax countries, despite negligible or limited business in that country.

They'll create multiple shell companies to disguise ownership.

They'll register patents and intellectual property in these low-tax countries and then pay themselves royalties there instead.

They'll play bureaucratic games and merge with smaller firms in low-tax countries to re-incorporate there for a lighter tax burden.

They'll implement pricing schemes to charge higher-tax countries more for goods and property.

And all this shit is completely legal.

Our government will panic and heavily slash corporate tax rates to try to get them back into this country, which of course brings us even *less* tax money from domestic businesses.

It must be the single greatest cause of lost revenue in history— Decades of Conservative policy eroding the burden for businesses, allowing them to rake in record profits without paying their share towards uplifting the society that allows their businesses to exist in the first place.

They don't use the lower taxes to lift wages or provide better benefits. They use it to build a golden mountain for the executives and top shareholders.

⚒ HOW WE COULD FIX IT ⚒

Obama tried to end the practice that allowed companies to defer profits to other countries, but Republicans and conservative Democrats blocked it every time.

Trump came in and implemented something called GILTI (Global Intangible Low-Taxed Income) which basically applied a minimum additional charge to foreign income that is taxed below a rate threshold.

Since the threshold was so low already and it was littered with loopholes (probably intentionally), it was a pretty sad attempt to patch the glitch.

Then there's the OECD, or the Organization for Economic Cooperation and Development, which is essentially a big-ass group of wealthy countries all getting together to instate a global minimum tax rate of 15% and implementing policies to reduce tax haven abuse.

So I guess there are already plans to try to fix this, but every effort needs a stronger push.

GILTI needs a higher minimum rate and to close loopholes. The OECD needs a tighter agreement. Companies need more public reporting requirements. The practice of shell companies and ownership secrecy frankly needs to be obliterated for these people. And we need punishing economic sanctions for countries that try to bend these rules.

To me it's just so irrational that this was ever allowed, and 15% still feels too low considering all the other financial games the wealthy and businesses play to avoid contributing to society.

Side note: There's a difference between using a shell company (like I've done) to protect the privacy of an individual from a witch hunt and using a shell company to hide profit centers and dodge taxes.

CORPORATE TAX BREAKS

In a similar vein of the "race-to-the-bottom" for the corporate rates that tax-haven countries use, there are also more local tax breaks that come in to play to even further reduce the burden for large companies.

This is when some huge business like Amazon or Apple or Tesla contacts various cities and initiates a bidding war to see who will offer the lowest rates to build a warehouse or a gigafactory or something.

TAXES

The companies will make a pile of promises about all the jobs they'll bring to the area, how much more money will flow in, how much more enticing and prosperous the city will be by mere virtue of the company's presence, yada yada.

In return, they'll get property tax reductions, sales tax reductions, corporate income tax reductions, payroll tax rebates, and heaps of other attractive incentives.

Meanwhile, there's no accountability or obligation for all the promises made in exchange for these tax breaks. Through hope alone, local taxpayers will foot the bill for all the infrastructure, housing, and other developments required to build and maintain that business.

Any benefit the company brings to the area is thoroughly eclipsed by the gigantic pile of lost tax revenue, and it all evaporates when that business decides to leave. Not to mention the other costs like intensified infrastructure strain, environmental damage, small business collapse, housing tensions, and more.

There's also industry-specific tax breaks like for oil tycoons, tech bro startups, real estate moguls, big-pharma "R&D", national sporting leagues, and more.

It's death by a thousand damn tax cuts.

And none of this ever trickles its way down to helping everyday Americans live happier, more affordable lives.

All it ever goes to is fucking stock buybacks and feeding the dragons.

Both Republicans and Democrats, but again largely Conservatives, are so invested in making companies pay as little as possible towards improving society.

It's socialist tax breaks for big businesses, funded by the rest of us.

⚒ HOW WE COULD FIX IT ⚒

We need more oversight on all of this, for one. These local tax-break bidding wars are ludicrous and need to stop. I don't have a solution for that other than making it outright illegal to offer companies over a certain size tax breaks at all.

Barring that, there needs to be more transparency and reporting on metrics like job creation and ROI. These companies need to foot the bill for infrastructure improvements necessitated by their existence. We need to continually audit these companies to ensure the cost-benefit analysis is proven accurate, and prevent them from doing shit like stock-buybacks while they're benefiting from any tax break.

We also need to look at what industries don't need any fucking tax incentives. Why does big oil need a tax break? Maybe give breaks to companies focusing on renewables, not for drilling more? Why does the public need to subsidize the construction of a football stadium? Why do depreciation deductions for real estate investors even exist?

It's such a mess. We just want healthcare, affordable housing, and comfortable lives. There's no money left for any of that, though.

THE IRS

The Conservative boogeyman. Or should I say their Baba Yaga?

The unhinged disgust that Conservatives have for the IRS is honestly hilarious. It's like they imagine a building packed full of Ferengi scheming and cackling as they prepare their next wave of audits.

The reality is they are just regular people trying to uphold the law.

If you're not a jackass when you call them, they are knowledgeable, cooperative, understanding of any mistakes, and will work with you to get things resolved. It's not their fault you screwed up on your taxes, but they do comprehend the complications and confusion.

The other reality Conservatives refuse to acknowledge is that the IRS has a phenomenally good return on investment, especially when you send them after the wealthier tax cheats.

It's something like every $1 spent on IRS enforcement yields $4-10 in recovered revenue. Insanely good returns.

But Conservatives just see government overreach and the unjust burden of taxes. They see how the poorer people are getting targeted for audits much more often, but not *why*. They see their politicians demonizing this organization as if it's some war against thieves and they get their pitchforks ready in April.

Why are Conservatives — the so-called party of "Law and Order" — so critical of an agency whose job is literally law enforcement?

Why are Conservatives — the so-called champions of small business and the working class — so keen on dulling the weapons that fight wealthy, lawyer-armed big businessmen and aristocrats?

Why are Conservatives — the so-called patrons of eliminating government waste — totally fine with the *hundreds of billions* of dollars in lost tax revenue *each year* due to false tax filings?

Because, Conservative leaders use the tax boogeyman as another anti-government scapegoat for their war against reason.

They tell their submissive supporters the government is stealing their money to pay for woke programs or whatever, they breed a strong distrust for both regulation and taxes, and they use this skepticism and the promise of a lower fiscal burden to secure votes.

The IRS is just another political punching bag for their usual rhetoric.

But the key is that weakening the IRS means that their wealthy peers don't have to worry as much about getting audited. They can keep gaming the system to dodge their dues.

"The IRS doesn't have the funds to challenge *my* legal team!"
evil laugh

If Conservative policy actually reflected the values they preach, they'd be championing the IRS as a tool for economic justice and a boon for the working class. Those aren't the marching orders though.

✖ HOW WE COULD FIX IT ✖

We should build a well-funded juggernaut of IRS agents and legal experts optimally equipped to audit the wealthy with relentless focus.

With a new, progressive tax code in place, the wealthy will be scrambling to find fresh avenues for tax avoidance.

If Conservatives insist on painting the IRS as a monster, then we should give them one.

FREE TAX FILING

And while we're talking about the IRS, let's not forget how crazy this country is about handling tax season.

Do y'all realize that in many other countries, the tax return is essentially already filled out, and all they have to do is review and sign?

It's free of both hassle and fees. It's simple.

And why exactly can't we have that? If you guessed "private lobbying-funded Conservative politicians within both parties but primarily Republicans blocking every attempt at reforms," then congratulations!

You win the sadness of awareness.

What these bastards would rather do is to kill free programs like Direct File and continue fellating the tax company execs with their usual oli-gargling gusto.

As I write this, they just made their move to officially end the IRS Direct File program — which was a free and easy way for regular people to submit their taxes.

Why would they do that? It's like they are comic book villains whose shitty superpower is privatizing everything.

✖ HOW WE COULD FIX IT ✖

We should adopt a similar pre-filled system that other developed countries have. This would help something like half of all taxpayers.

For everyone else, implement a robust, easy to use, publicly-funded, *free* tax-filing system. Also offer plentiful tools for those struggling to fill things out accurately.

If people still want to go off and use some tax professional or accountant or whatever for assistance, fine. But intentionally exterminating the free option is just so stupid and evil.

And we can't forget to use both hands to flip the bird to those tax-filing companies that flood Congress with lobbyists.

CLOSING RANT

My mom once asked me, "Why are you complaining about all of this if it's something you are going to benefit from when we die?"

Well for one, my parents' holdings aren't worth anywhere near anything remotely close to limits like the Lifetime Exemption, and most of the changes I would want to see would not be impacting my meager inheritance much. I *might* be able to pay down my mortgage and have a little extra to work with each month. It's not life-altering.

Secondly, I *want* things to get better for the country. I would *want* to pay more in taxes if it meant my family could have more affordable healthcare, my kid's education would be better, etc. etc.

It's that hilarious Boomer Conservative selfish mentality that just because I may *slightly* benefit from some mercenary, asinine, broken system that I shouldn't want to fix it. I want to fix it!

Even back in the "great" days of higher top-end income tax rates, the wealthy used a maze of loopholes to get around paying their fair share. This shit needed to be fixed eons ago.

Just imagine how much better the country, or really the world, would be if the wealthy weren't so hellbent on rigging the game and actually paid their dues to society.

The top 1% of households are sitting on something like *$43 TRILLION* in assets. It's enough to quite probably solve many of the world's troubles given time and focus.

We do not have a resource shortage problem. We have a resource *distribution* problem.

I *know* that truly taxing the wealthy like this would be like playing whack-a-mole.

They'll do anything to keep hiding and hoarding. We'd have to stay on top of it and close as many new loopholes as we can to make sure they are paying their taxes.

I'm not an accountant, and I'm not knowledgeable enough to predict all the tricks they'd use, but we have to try *something*.

Just because it would be difficult to fix, Conservatives vote as if we shouldn't try anything at all and instead brown-nose the wealthy like they're in the will.

Would Conservatives complain so much about taxes if it was more obvious that the wealthy actually contribute an equitable share to the societal pot?

Would they still scream about *socialism* if their visit to the ER was free, or if their kid's college was free, or if their town's infrastructure was up to date, or if this country was actually great for the working class?

I mean...probably...they always seem to have *something* complain about. But maybe they'd whisper more.

HEALTHCARE

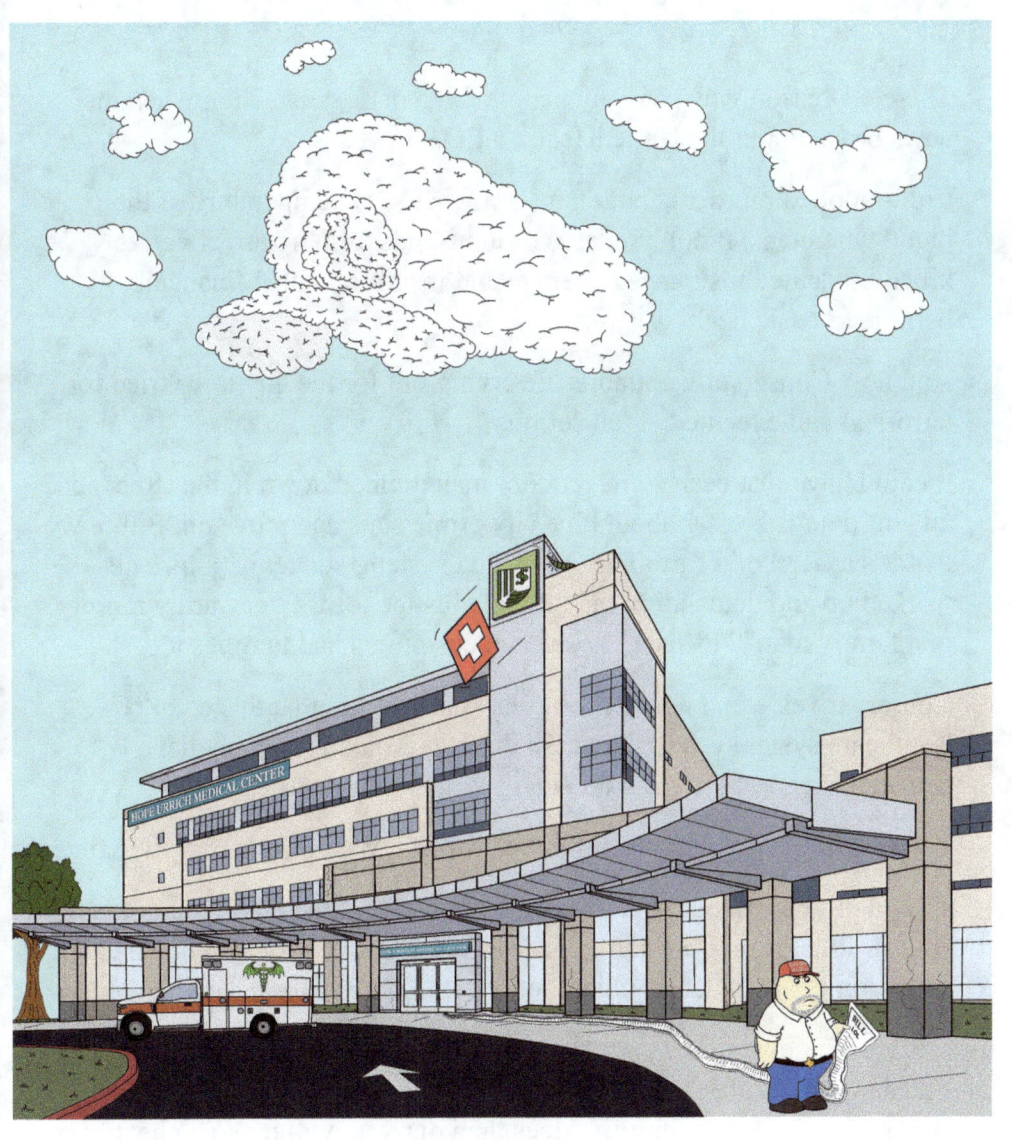

HEALTHCARE

There's a reason why so many people felt a dark satisfaction when the news broke about the UnitedHealth CEO.

Cold-blooded murder is not okay. But what's the temperature of the blood when tens, if not hundreds of thousands or more are effectively killed by denied insurance coverage and insurmountable financial barriers to basic healthcare?

And now Conservative pundits are crying out for the guy to be tried for terrorism and executed. Y'all serious?

It could have just been some random man gunned down in the street and all you'd do is bluster about blue city crime stats and move on. But now that it's a CEO of a cartoonishly wicked system, suddenly you're all worked up and demanding the ultimate justice for the "cowardly murder of a family man"? Please. Those dead customers had families too.

Conservatives, you know in your blackened hearts that this country's healthcare system is a nightmarish disaster. You all probably have personal anecdotes to back up what you know to be true.

You can stop defending the ultra-wealthy that will never suffer the same.

They don't care about you. They don't care about the quality or cost of your healthcare, or your family's healthcare, or your friends' healthcare. They don't care about anything but watching the stock price line go up and to the right.

You can join us Progressives in our call for changes to this deplorable system. It won't burn, and if it does then our way will make it cheaper and easier to get treatment.

SINGLE-PAYER HEALTHCARE

Is there any regular person out there that's like, "Oh my health benefits are amazing, reliable, and worth the cost"? Shit I'd be surprised if even wealthier people were thrilled with private health insurance.

I have numerous minor health issues that I'd love to see a doctor about. But despite the fact that I have "decent" health insurance through my employer which costs me over $500 a freaking month for me and my partner to get the bare bones coverage, it is still so expensive to go out and seek treatment for things.

It's agonizing seeing how much I pay for health insurance, knowing that all it will really do is help me not become medically bankrupt in an emergency. That is, only if the stars align and all the professionals that treat me in this hypothetical emergency follow every inane rule that the insurance gods command.

Meanwhile other developed nations get to flaunt their nationalized healthcare and the hospital bills where the parking fee was the most expensive part of a two-week stay.

I *want* to go to the doctor more often the older I get. It's just so unreasonably expensive, and the bill would only make my stress worse.

Our country's health insurance system is a fucking abomination and Conservatives on both sides are largely to blame.

We've tried a few times to pass a single-payer system or to at least take the first steps down that path, and every time it's Conservatives that have fought against its implementation. Every time, it's the combination of private industry lobbying and the Conservatives in Congress doing everything they can to block such legislation. Even Medicare and Medicaid had fierce Conservative opposition when first implemented.

Republicans are out here arguing to *keep* medical debt on people's credit scores, because of course they are!

They've always used the term "socialized medicine" to scare their base into rejecting a single-payer system. Wanting to give people access to truly affordable healthcare is *SOCIALISM!* *scary progressive noises*

Even when Congress offers band-aid solutions to our defective system, Republicans play their traditional fearmongering games — like they did with "OBAMACARE".

Fox and the like branded the Affordable Care Act, which was largely an attempt to get more of the country insured and to eliminate coverage denial for things like preexisting conditions, as "Obamacare" to scare their aging and ailing base into thinking it was bad for them. And, go figure, it worked.

They went around saying, "Oh Obamacare is so bad, that's why I'm on the Affordable Care Act." That's some chef's kiss Conservative awareness right there.

Meanwhile as I write this, the GOP-controlled house just passed a measure that severely guts Medicaid.

Why have so many other countries — poorer countries, less powerful countries — *ALL* figured this shit out already and the U.S. hasn't?

No. We *do* have it figured out. The powers at play *know* we could do it. They just don't want to spend the time, and more importantly the *money*.

An unfathomable fortune of lobbying from private insurers and an equally unfathomable record of corruption, shortsightedness, and stupidity from our legislators has kept the status quo of our contemptible healthcare system firmly in place.

So while all the Congressional opponents of true universal healthcare get to enjoy a lifetime of socialized medicine and government benefits using our fucking tax dollars, the rest of us suffer and die under the gold-plated, gem-laden boot of privatized health.

I have a friend that had some kind of serious health event that left him needing immediate medical care. He had to go to the ER right away, yet he was afraid to call an ambulance because he simply couldn't afford it. Drove himself. What a travesty. What a damn broken system.

I'd wager that nearly all four people that'll read this worthless book have similar anecdotes highlighting the miserable failings of U.S. healthcare.

Too many Americans are one adverse health event away from ruin.

And Conservatives continue to keep it that way. They consistently vote for policies that make this shit worse, and vote down policies that aim to make things better for everyday people.

They'd rather pay the enormous landfill of additional overhead costs, line the pockets of wealthy businessmen, and defend a system that leaves millions to die of manageable diseases than establish nationalized medicine for all.

I commonly complain to my parents about this particular aggravation.

I'll tell my mom about some health concern. She'll tell me to see a doctor about it. And then I divulge how much it would cost me, and I just can't stomach the price. My dad then says, without a shred of irony or empathy, "Well I'm on Medicare now and it's great!"

Yeah, no kidding, I bet it is! Asshole.

"I paid for it my whole working life! I deserve it!" he says.

Hang on, let's really stop and think about how insane that mindset is.

You work for 45+ years of your life and are effectively forced to pay for incredibly expensive private health insurance plans with disappointing, confusing coverage — I'm talking paying hundreds of thousands of dollars to private healthcare companies on just the *premiums* over the course of your working life.

You need to see? That's extra. You need your teeth not to rot? That's extra. You need some drugs? Yeah, we'll see about that. You have an emergency? We'll cover a little of it I guess, but you gotta pay your outlandish deductible first! We're gonna argue with your doctor about it regardless! Need therapy? Just don't be sad! It's not covered!

Then there's the co-pays, the co-insurance, the various bullshit fees, the stuff you *thought* was covered but isn't, on and on and on.

And all the while in that depressing time, you are *also* paying FICA taxes to cover a socialized medicine system that, if you even make it to 65, you'll only get to use for another 15 or so years.

I mean the average life expectancy in the U.S. is like 78 years and dropping! You'd be above average to get 15 years out of it!

Now here you are, effectively paying for two separate health care plans. One that barely covers anything, fights your doctor, fights you, and still leaves you burdened by debt and terrified to visit the doctor for *anything*, and another plan that you don't even get to benefit from until you are old, withered from work, and looking at death on the horizon.

But hey — Conservatives are thrilled with all this, yeah? They sure vote like they are!

And what's even worse about this system is that Medicare isn't even that good compared to other socialized systems!

It still has high out of pocket costs. You have to get expensive supplemental plans through goddamn private health insurance for things like dental, vision, and drugs.

Like…it still kind of sucks even after everything you've put into it!

HEALTHCARE

It's FUBAR. Yet another disaster brought to you by Conservative ideology, the voracity of politicians, and their manipulative rhetoric.

This one, however, is a both-parties disaster. Only true Progressives are out there calling for a universal health plan like the UK's NHS.

Of course, even the Conservatives across the pond are doing everything they can to dismantle the NHS. Does the NHS have difficulties? Yup. Are most of those difficulties a direct result of concentrated Conservative efforts to severely weaken the NHS? Also yup.

It's the classic Conservative playbook: break a functioning system so they can then complain about why it doesn't work.

You Conservatives must be overwhelmingly healthy people then, right? Why else would you work against fixing our healthcare system? You must not need doctors!

Wait, that's not right. Red states have higher rates of chronic illness, have lower life expectancy, *and* have worse access to healthcare than Blue states? Shoot, if only there was a set of policies that could shrink those gaps!

And here's another layer to this mess. What kind of fucking dumbass government would refuse to do everything it can to keep its citizens as healthy as possible?

Do our best and brightest on Capitol Hill truly not understand that part of having a happy, strong, and *productive* society is for people to be healthy in both mind and body? People need to be *alive and well* to produce widgets and provide services and empower a nation. Seems like a goddamn obvious first step to an enviable society.

Conservatives must believe that the "free" market gives us the best healthcare in the world though, yeah? That's what they say on their news shows! Our healthcare costs our entire savings, but it's unsurpassed!

So, does our current system then boast the best health outcomes in the world considering it demands over double what the countries with nationalized healthcare spend?

Oh…

Life expectancy? 5-10 years lower
Infant mortality? Twice as high
Maternal mortality? Three to six times higher
Preventable hospitalizations? Higher
Readmissions? Higher
Infectious disease mortality? Higher
Chronic disease mortality? Higher
Suicide rates? Higher

And the list could go on. Our outcomes suck! We spend so much more money on healthcare, and we don't even get the best in the world!

To be clear, it's not our doctors. Our professionals are plenty skilled.

It's abysmal access to affordable healthcare.

It's people like me actively avoiding the doctor to get various concerns checked out because we are worried about the cost.

It's letting issues go unseen and unspoken for so long that they become chronic, costly conditions.

It's taking an Uber instead of an ambulance.

It's unaffordable prenatal care.

It's being the only developed country without guaranteed parental leave.

It's the burdensome stress induced by insurance profiteering.

It's the poverty imposed on us by the wealthy elite.

It's Conservative policy.

🛠 HOW WE COULD FIX IT 🛠

I mean the only answer is the merciless and exhaustive dismantling of every private health insurance network from top to bottom and the installment of a national health insurance program. Give it a catchy title like "Medicare For All". Or you know, maybe just Medicare. That's the answer. Always has been.

We already pay grotesque, bank-breaking premiums for healthcare when we could pay even less for a national system. Bernie has been lecturing about that for a long time and he's absolutely right, as usual. He's right!

Stop being okay with giving your money to a private health insurer that is just going to deny your annual physical exam, and give it to a national plan that will make the exam feel free and encouraged!

Let doctors be doctors and stop wasting their time and energy battling insurance companies and what some shitty AI or an underpaid, overworked pencil-pusher considers best health practices.

It's not like any change will happen overnight. It'd be slow, grueling, and some billionaires might lose a yacht or two in the process. But it's change that needed to happen long ago and Conservatives need to stop supporting policies that do nothing but hasten the deaths of their lives and bank accounts.

We need healthcare, not wealthcare.

PRESCRIPTION DRUG PRICES

This is categorically related to the nationalized health insurance argument but is also worth mentioning on its own.

Conservatives have consistently voted against policies that would allow the government to negotiate for better drug pricing models. They'll go on and on about letting the "free" market dictate prices while they watch the pharma lobby write their campaign checks.

Since when has the "free" market ever done what's best for the consumer? We're talking about *health* here, not a freaking iPhone.

These drug companies care about profit alone. They profit from your ailments, they profit from overprescribed medications, and they profit from paying our government officials to look the other way on their heartless exploitations.

Once again, this is a both-parties frustration. Still, Republicans have had a noticeable bias towards crippling the government's group purchasing power and forcing citizens to pay crazy prices for indispensable drugs.

I mean look at what they did with insulin — something that costs barely anything to make and is a supremely critical medication.

Biden enacted a $35 cap on insulin (only for Medicare recipients and still too expensive), and when his administration tried to extend that cap to private health insurance holders as well, Senate Republicans blocked it. Deplorable. And now, under the second Trump administration, they are trying to remove that $35 cap for Medicare recipients too. Because of course they are! It's the evil thing to do!

That's just one example, but I have to wonder how many Conservatives on insulin even know about that? If the yapping millionaire propagandists didn't tell them about it, I doubt they'd realize until reading the receipt at the pharmacy.

Then they'd blame Biden and the Democrats for the drain to their livelihood, no doubt.

Countries with nationalized healthcare are able to become a giant Group Purchasing Organization and negotiate for much lower prices on nearly everything. We have GPOs in the U.S. too, but the scope of their discounts pales in comparison to that of a nationalized health system.

Drug companies instead exploit the U.S. and our horribly corrupt system to extract every ounce of value they can out of dirt-cheap medications.

They'll do this under the shroud of "Research and Development", but what that really means is patent lawyers. Making tiny, probably useless adjustments to various medications so they can renew rights and keep charging a fortune. And our government just lets them.

⚒ HOW WE COULD FIX IT ⚒

I mean in an ideal scenario I'd nationalize the drug manufacturers too, at the very least for a large formulary of the most commonly-needed and prescribed medications.

The U.S. could create its own drug compounding enterprise to become a primary provider of these medications. Just make it our damn selves and stop relying on private, profit-driven companies for everything.

Anything too cost ineffective for public manufacturers could use the new universal healthcare system's leverage to negotiate lower prices for this formulary of drugs.

We could periodically evaluate new drugs that should be on this formulary and update the list of drugs we should produce ourselves.

It's also worth looking at the patent laws for many drugs and removing the layers and layers of bullshit current companies use to shield their inexorable greed.

It's downright inhumane — the burden some of these medications cost people, many of whom are at the mercy of genetics alone.

Conservatives care about those blonde-haired, blue-eyed, big-tittied genes, not the kind that make you sick. Those genes are *your* fault.

Again, the government should be striving to keep its citizens healthy if it wants to remain a superpower.

You'd think Conservative lawmakers would understand that you can't govern corpses.

<u>MENTAL HEALTH</u>

Getting treated for mental health issues is sometimes seen as a luxury. I've heard therapy described as "rich people shit" because it's so expensive and often not covered under health plans. Even when it *is* covered to some degree it can still feel too expensive to get even the most rudimentary counseling services.

When I went to therapy it was a $30 copay per visit, once a week. Doesn't sound like much, yet recall that my benefits cost me like $500+ a month for me and my partner, and they were considered "good". I could afford it, but $120 a month is a lot for people.

And I frankly quit going partly on account of that expense. I just couldn't justify it. I'd say I was "not that bad" and move on. That's not healthy behavior! Look at this asinine book I'm writing instead!

Mental health disorders are an epidemic at this point because Boomers didn't take it seriously. Their "treatments" for mental health irregularities, ranging from high-functioning autistic behavior to full-on debilitating neurodivergence, were always somewhere on a spectrum between ignoring it and trying to electrocute it out of you.

Maybe it's not all their fault because *their* parents certainly didn't have a good grasp on it either. There's always been a stigma associated with mental health, and their misunderstanding of the science just meant they didn't care to address it.

But there's this weird thing we can do as humans called learning and adapting and improving. It appears those concepts are particularly hard for Conservatives to understand because they are also consistently voting to cut or prevent coverage for mental health services.

The ACA put mental health treatments under an "essential services" category, which, go figure, Republicans opposed. Granted they opposed just about everything the ACA tried to do.

But they had *eight years* of Obama's presidency to come up with something new for when Trump 1.0 took office and they came up with nothing. They couldn't get past their in-party bickering and had no plan to "fix" anything. No doubt Trump 2.0 will get right on that.

Mental health support is a repeatedly cut program when budget-slicing happens. It's so short-sighted and ignores a critical aspect of a thriving population's health and wellness. Not to mention our veterans very often need mental health treatments to work through trauma related to their service. Or is PTSD woke shit now?

It's always Progressive/Leftist policies pushing for mental health support by including it in universal healthcare coverage, boosting access to services, and/or advocating programs to reduce the stigma associated with mental health conditions.

Conservatives, on the other hand, use mental health illnesses as a tool. They use it to fortify profit margins for private health insurers. They use it to push for more law enforcement power. They use it as a scapegoat for gun violence to avoid actually fucking doing something about gun violence. Thoughts and prayers, y'all!

Conservative budgets leave no room at all for mental health. They don't *want* to spend the money treating it.

They want "individual responsibility" instead of working together as a society to help and heal these people.

🛠 HOW WE COULD FIX IT 🛠

We add comprehensive mental health support to the universal healthcare plan (whatever name it gets).

We'd start covered services at a very young age, and expand counseling resources (and other needs) to schools and communities.

We can also increase funding for researching psychological ailments and treatment methods.

I do believe that alleviating the stresses of poverty as discussed in the Capitalism section of these rants would go an incredibly long way to improving the country's mental health. That combined with better access to low-cost physical healthcare would do wonders.

It's wild how far just "not being so anxious about money all the time" can go to helping people feel better. For everything else, identifying concerns early on and providing inexpensive, effective care needs to be a priority.

ABORTION

Oh look, I put this doozy in the Healthcare section of my rambling book.

Why did I do that, Conservatives?

Is it…is it because it's a healthcare decision?

A decision made between a woman and her doctor? A decision made while considering the physical, mental, and financial health of the patient who is facing the pregnancy and its consequences?

Why yes that *is* why it's in the Healthcare section!

Boy do Conservatives love a good rallying cry for the unborn. Yet their policies don't portray any concern about the health and wellbeing of these babies *after* they're born, and they certainly don't fret over the health of the mothers. But while that kiddo is growing in the womb, it sure is valuable to them!

Women should be treated as more than just incubation chambers.

I'm not going to insert that little speech about the unborn by that pastor, Dave Barnhart, but it's worth looking up as its relevance hasn't changed.

It notes that abortion is used by the Right as advocacy for "all life" being sacred, and they cry out that the Bible would label abortion as murder. The Bible never explicitly supports or condemns abortion at all, but Conservatives are good at ignoring the inconvenient words in that book.

Their party platform is not pro-life in the slightest. Their policies create a system that is pro-war, pro-famine, pro-poverty, and pro-suffering.

They are also supposed to be the party of "small government" but this silly book is riddled with examples that show how hollow that claim is.

Conservatives eagerly vote to allow the federal government to intrude upon your personal life and dictate what you can and can't do, including forcing someone to give birth even if they were assaulted, suffer from health conditions, or are simply too poor to properly care for the child.

Like with many stances right-wing leaders take, abortion is just another tool to influence their supporters, and a noticeably effective one.

Many Republicans will proudly distinguish themselves as pro-life champions. They'll say, "Hey, fellow Christians! Look! We ban abortion everywhere we can! We rage against programs like Planned Parenthood! We advocate abstinence instead of educating on safe practices!"

Meanwhile they will cut funding for childcare and schools, fight against the right to healthcare, give billionaires tax cuts to exacerbate poverty, and enact an onslaught of policies that worsen the hardships of life.

Abortion is such a divisive topic that it speaks loudly to a particular group of folks called "single-issue voters".

You know, the sort of people living in a magical bubble that provides them the privilege to ignore all the other atrocities going on, all the other important issues, all the nuance, and all the critical thought needed in deciding who to vote for.

They'll trumpet, "Well I am pro-life, so I always vote Republican."

Such a mystical bubble where nothing but the rights the unborn really matters. I've personally seen a few of these bubbles in my life.

Abortion is also one of the many subjects where that classic tenet of Conservatism is observed. The old hypocrisy of "well it's okay now that it affects *me.*"

If you are a certain type of Conservative, it is *imperative* that you do *not* care about something until it impacts you directly. So please, go out there and protest a woman's right to bodily autonomy.

But if, heaven forbid, the day ever comes when your own daughter faces an unthinkable situation, go ahead and quietly swap your stance behind closed doors to keep her safe.

Take heed and do it privately, because you're right back out there on the picket line after your daughter recovers, okay? The pro-life champions need your continued support!

As smarter people have put it — "The only moral abortion is my own".

I could maybe… *maybe*… give pro-lifers a little more credit for their stance on the sanctity of life if the rest of the platform they voted for supported that stance at all.

But it doesn't. So they get zero points for effort.

🛠 HOW WE COULD FIX IT 🛠

We make abortion 100% legal in certified health facilities under the supervision of licensed health practitioners.

We improve the quality and quantity of women's services to assist mothers with pregnancies and other women's health issues.

We mandate and refine, or implement, sex education and relevant resources to public schools and other institutions to guide people towards making the best decisions they can, with the most medically accurate information available.

Then I guess we watch as new children grow up happier and healthier in homes that want them.

VACCINES

This isn't a uniquely Conservative-born crisis. There are plenty of Liberals out there peddling their own ignorant, anti-science views. I just wanted to add this section because Conservatives let a propagator of dangerous, fallacious, anti-vax word vomit head the DHHS.

He's out there claiming he's going to get to bottom of the "autism epidemic" in a couple months of work, he's removing CDC members that advise on vaccines, and he's cutting hundreds of millions in funding for vaccine research. He and his policies are a threat to public health.

Conservatives also have a storied history with cynicism towards professionals and scientists that have enough integrity to live in reality.

Just look at their overall response to Covid-19. That pandemic very publicly exposed how many fucking selfish crybabies we have in this country. Wearing masks and getting vaccinated to protect your fellows against a fairly deadly virus was just too much of a violation of their personal liberties.

Conservatives are still, to this day, declaring that Dr. Anthony Fauci, who has been a public health servant for decades and did his job admirably with the available information, deserves the ultimate punishment for "crimes against humanity" during his role in advising the nation through the pandemic.

Remember, to them it's people like Luigi that deserve the death penalty.

These anti-vaxxers cling to their survivorship bias and shriek in a liberal-mocking tone, "My body, my choice!" as they refuse to bolster the herd immunity of a nation. They have such a profound and harmful ignorance of the fucking point of vaccines, while their selfishness transcends the bounds of morality and a sense of communal duty.

They take the word of a discredited, license-less doctor conducting a deeply flawed and manipulated study with only twelve subjects to prove a link between vaccines and autism. And they simultaneously ignore the many extensive studies with literally millions of subjects showing no links to autism whatsoever.

The misinformation flooding from social media scientists selling unregulated supplement pills and "vitamin" water is somehow given so much credibility that diseases are returning from near-extinction — Measles, Mumps, Polio, Whooping Cough, Rubella, Diphtheria…

It must be such a blissful existence. To have the luxury of not dying from preventable diseases because so many others around you are sheltering you by getting immunized. To have no understanding of the millions of deaths it took to get to this point of biological protection. Well not anymore, assholes. Your kids are in trouble now!

Vaccines. Fucking. *Work.* They *WORK*!

They do *not* cause autism. There is no grand world domination mind-control plan. There are no 5G microchip nanobots swimming in the syringe. We have generations of proof and a list of vanquished diseases to show that vaccines and herd immunity work extremely well.

Like I said, not a uniquely right-wing setback, but they distinctly don't help with their passionate and outspoken distrust of actual scientific experts or with their elevation of unqualified, deadly dipshits to the top health offices in the country.

Granted, elevating unqualified dipshits to top offices *is* one area where Conservatives have shown impressive talent.

We saw exactly how much trust they place in qualified scientists during Covid-19. Those horse-pill chuggers would have rather choked on vet-approved Ivermectin and died than listen to anyone other than their propagandists about how to handle the situation.

You can lead a horse to water, but you can't make him put on a goddamn mask and get vaccinated.

⚒ HOW WE COULD FIX IT ⚒

There's nothing to fix except public perception, I guess?

Vaccines are not broken. They are modern miracles.

Maybe start by never again nominating these MD-free, compromised clowns to lead in the country's health-related decisions?

Could also hold people legally accountable for spreading such harmful disinformation, but that might get the free speech absolutists in a tizzy. Considering this dumb book might get me deported, maybe I should remain on team free speech.

Really the best method we've got to fix this anti-vax dilemma is to focus on the new generation of children.

Foster scientific curiosity and critical thinking.

Correct any courseloads that fail to highlight the importance of vaccines, and advocate for other fundamental educational shifts that will bring the next generation admiration for these wonders of medicine.

Teach about bias, illustrate the power of manipulated statistics, and discuss the differences between strong studies and flawed ones so they can spot bullshit when it pops up in their doom scrolling.

If an educated populace also had a strong government that instilled confidence in experts and science, maybe the anti-vax crowd would be mocked as loudly as the flat-earthers are. At least those buffoons aren't hurting anyone but Big Globe, though.

Anti-vaxxers lead to the revitalization of would-be eradicated diseases and they compromise millions of vulnerable people. It's a serious public health crisis and needs adequate cultural and educational resistance.

ADVERTISEMENT OF PHARMACEUTICALS

Did you know that the U.S. and New Zealand are the only countries in the *world* that allow direct-to-consumer advertising of pharmaceuticals?

I mean I knew the U.S. did, obviously. Can't watch anything without being inundated by, "Ask your doctor about Raptoricil, the only drug pending FDA approval for treating restless bowel syndrome caused by overconsumption of Dino Nuggets! Side effects include death."

I didn't go to medical school for eight years with four whatever years of residency. Why would I ignore the expertise of doctors and pharmacists in preference to what privately-owned pharma companies want me to do for treatment? It's wild that I would get input at all into what drugs are ideal for my situation. Yet there are people out there pretending like they know better because the ads work a little too well on them.

I'm not saying that general awareness of treatment options is a bad thing, but just you know…do what the commercials always say and *talk* to your doctor about your problems. They likely either know what to do or at least know what sources to use to find the right treatment for you. They really don't need your input beyond symptoms.

It makes the doctor's job harder and it adds costs throughout the system. How much money do you think goes into advertising? You pay for that.

And here we are again, with progressive Democrats pushing for outright bans of this practice and conservative Republicans gobbling up lobbying money and blocking every attempt at improving the system. They call out "free market!" and "freedom of speech!" and other frankly irrelevant arguments so they can please their donors.

This is a health issue, and misleading or confusing pharmaceutical ads do not always promote effective treatments.

REGULATION OF SUPPLEMENTS

This is a personal soapbox inclusion here, but it's still healthcare.

131

It's a Conservative-critical topic in that they have such a raging obsession with deregulation, and Progressives are the only ones calling for any reform here.

It was, surprisingly, a bipartisan bill that allowed the supplement industry to break loose, and it passed with overwhelming support owing to staggering amounts of lobbying.

The bill was called the Dietary Supplement Health and Education Act, and it said that supplements can be treated as food.

They didn't need pre-market approval by the FDA, companies could make vague claims about what the supplements were supposed to actually *do*, and the FDA couldn't do squat until *after* the supplement actually hurt someone.

It's worth mentioning that the public generally supported this policy too. The logic is that "Big Pharma is evil" and supplement companies out to make an enormous fortune selling sugar pills and snake oils are uh…are not evil…I guess.

Ever since the bill passed, the supplement industry has exploded beyond belief. I'm talking tens of billions of dollars annually, and it just keeps growing and growing.

You've got everyone from social media fitness "gurus" to right-wing podcasting incel quacks peddling supplements for damn near everything — cancer blockers, dick enlargers, fat melters, you name it.

I don't actually care about that, necessarily — if people want to throw down their life savings on ox bile and moon dust then I guess go ahead.

The problem I have is when companies get away with outright lying to consumers about the effects of this "food", or worse when the supplements actually have dangerous chemicals, banned substances, or even undisclosed drugs in them.

Some of these pills have lasting, damaging effects on people!

Companies will get an FDA recall order and then do nothing to fix the offense before putting it back on the shelves. They'll use tacky labelling tricks and pay "influencers" to peddle their wares to a highly targeted audience. They'll even inspire cruel hunting practices to harvest animal parts with no scientifically valid benefits.

There's such little oversight into protecting consumers at all — at least not until after it's too late for some.

Well now we get excess supplement-related liver failures, we have the elderly taking prescriptions with a minefield of unknown supplement interactions, and even children being fed supplements as alternatives to real medicine.

That is the problem I have.

It's a healthcare headache first, a capitalism conundrum second, and it needs to be regulated.

✖ HOW WE COULD FIX IT ✖

What I want is for the government to fund solid research into these supplements, to require pre-market approval, to create a compulsory registration system similar to the National Drug Code standards, to require batch/lot info for traceability, to impose stronger labeling rules (like drug interactions and side effects), and to mandate independent testing to verify ingredient accuracy.

I also want to enforce these regulations and punish companies for false advertising, contamination offenses, and fraudulent research. Any companies with a history of problems deserve to be treated as public health hazards and shut down.

Yet what we currently have is a Conservative-dominated government that's crippling the power of the FDA, dismantling consumer protections, and hawking the "benefits" of raw milk.

So, naturally, the exact opposite of what's best for our health.

CLOSING RANT

We *could* have universal healthcare. We *could* have cheaper prescription drugs. We *could* have comprehensive mental health coverage. We *could* have the right to make healthcare decisions that affect only our own bodies. We *could* continue eradicating preventable diseases. We *could* have stronger rules guiding the treatments available to us.

We could have it all, but instead we have a nation where many cheer at the murder of a healthcare CEO.

We have theocratic dystopian policies trying to track pregnant women and prevent their right to choose.

We have once-exterminated diseases writing comeback stories.

We have ineffective alternative medicine being cheaper and more appealing than true treatment.

We have billionaire capitalists telling millionaire legislators telling destitute voters that nothing can be done.

And Conservative voters are apparently delighted with all that.

EDUCATION

DEPARTMENT OF
EDUCATION

EDUCATION

It's no surprise that the platform of stupidity and evil would be such a stubborn opposing force to intelligence and education.

Conservative leadership "love the poorly educated" because an uninformed electorate is easy to dupe, easy to rally, and easy to control. The propaganda they rely on so heavily — the disinformation, the buzzwords, the bigotry, the thoughtless patriotism — all require a voting bloc that is largely lacking in critical thought and other skills that a strong education can nurture.

The Republicans are the party of banning books.

They are the party of sanitizing history in favor of misplaced pride.

They are the party that severs school funding and attacks teachers.

They are the party that prioritizes faith over facts.

They are the party that derides college and limits its accessibility.

They are the party that denies science and experts with fervor.

They are the party that would rather leave school children vulnerable to hunger and violence than offer comfort and safety in the classroom.

They are the party that sends us falling back and back and back while other developed nations continue to strengthen their access to education and raise smarter kids.

Then the Conservatives scratch those itchy heads and wonder why America is losing its greatness.

Today, Conservative leadership and policies continue to undermine educational institutions in every way imaginable — from cutting funds to outright expelling foreign students. Meanwhile, other countries swoop in and offer these bright and talented individuals a better future, accelerating America's intellectual downfall.

Not like there will be any rocket scientists left here for long, but this isn't rocket science anyway. If you don't invest in the health and education of your population, they will either perish early or be on average dumber than the population of a country that chose the much wiser investment.

Conservative groups are not known for carefully evaluating the long-term impact of any of their policies, and it is no more evident than in their treatment of education.

As in all things —

They see short-term financial gain to the wealthy few.

They see short-term political points towards their next election.

They see short-term solutions to every long-term problem.

There's a theory out there that the Conservative elite schemers, like the Project 2025 Heritage Foundation, do all of this on purpose — that they champion anti-intellectualism to not only reduce human lifespan, but to ensure a steady supply of thoughtless laborers whose lives are only as valuable as the money they generate to the oligarchs.

Can't take retirement benefits if you're dead, after all.

I'm not sure if they are actually capable of such masterminding, but perhaps some of those intelligent, evil people pulling the strings could craft such a plan.

It doesn't really matter if it's on purpose or not. It's happening under Conservative leadership regardless and it needs to be stopped.

Or else this country will continue its agonizing descent into idiocracy.

PROPERTY TAXES AND SCHOOL SUCCESS

What crystal-clear proof that this country wants only the wealthiest children to receive the most educational capital available. Tying property taxes to school funding is a detestable practice.

We need to scrap the belief that the wealthier neighborhoods should automatically get the very best schools. It's abhorrent classism and it's clearly deliberate.

I put this in the Conservative bucket because they are consistently the ones resisting any reform to this unfair system. Progressives are often pushing for a more equalized system that aggregates the funds from things like property taxes and spreads that wealth evenly among the schools — Usually at least on a state level.

We have this continuous loop where poorer neighborhoods have poorer schools, so the students have lower graduation rates and harsher chances of getting into college, which means they earn less income and have to move to a poorer neighborhood where they raise poorer children...and the wheel keeps turning.

It's a cycle of poverty, this trap that exists in part because schools in poorer areas just don't get the same educational advantages. It's not the kids' fault and they deserve a better policy.

Funding should be allocated based on need, not on wealth. Take all the property and local taxes in the state that are allocated for education and distribute the funds with calculated care to financial privilege.

And — weird take here — maybe property taxes don't have to be the primary driver for school funding?

If we taxed the fucking rich more then we could have more federal-level funds available for improving education across the board.

TEACHER SALARIES

In many states, mainly Red ones, teachers earn what is considered to be low class wages. Some teachers will work second jobs and side hustles like OnlyFans just to make ends meet. They are required to get a degree — and sometimes even a master's — just to get competitive pay, which means likely facing student debt.

Conservatives regularly treat teachers as non-essential and disposable, probably because the field is skewed toward women and people of color — two groups their bigotry never hesitates to devalue. And in their dependable distaste for all non-police unions, Conservatives will also furiously fight against the demands of teachers' unions.

Teaching is one of the most noble professions out there. It is such an immensely important job for guiding the future of a nation through its youth. They deserve support. They deserve resources. And they deserve to get paid a truly generous salary for all they do.

Yes, some teachers suck in the same way that some cops suck or some politicians suck or some business analysts suck or some contractors suck, etc. So to Conservatives, because a handful of teachers may not deserve extra pay, we should screw over all the good teachers too!

If you can't tell, this is a very common mindset for them — to deny helping the whole because of the actions of a miniscule minority.

Many people that may *want* to teach avoid it simply because it is so thankless and pays like shit. How many motivated, qualified, and truly skilled would-be educators have evaded the profession entirely because of this neglect?

If teacher salaries (and education funding in general) increase, then the profession will attract the brightest, most passionate graduates out there, schools can then be more selective about who they hire because they have more and more applicants for jobs, the overall quality of education across the country rises, and we see all academic metrics climb to meet the best-taught nations of the world.

It's so obvious it hurts.

ADMINISTRATIVE BLOAT

This isn't really a Conservative thing, it just pisses me off.

Many teachers have voiced their intense frustration for the administrative waste in schools — for the layers and layers of bureaucracy and management who are all likely to earn more than the average teacher.

Imagine how disheartening that must be if you were a teacher, pouring your soul into educating these kids and getting told you have to fund your own supplies by some middle management school board asshole that makes three times what you do for a fraction of the work.

When we reform education, we need to do some administrative culling and even things out, like any business overloaded with worthless yet overpaid positions should.

School districts need to focus on improving the lives and efficacy of the workers that directly impact student outcomes, not the hollow-titled drones in admin.

We need to audit these non-teaching roles for usefulness and cap admin-to-teacher salary ratios.

FREE SCHOOL MEALS

Imagine proudly supporting the team that denies poor children the right to be adequately fed during school. Go team.

Conservatives have fought against policies that seek to provide free meals to school children for as long as I can remember. This one debate is an excellent microcosm example of everything wrong with Conservative ideology, really. It's perfect.

For starters, it's cruel.

The crushing weight of unregulated capitalism has caused hard-working, well-meaning parents to rely on school lunches to ease the financial burden of feeding their kids during the day. But Conservatives just can't resist taking away every little thing that helps low-income families.

They see free school lunches as another form of welfare and a waste of their precious tax dollars. They fret about the "wrong people" getting aid and vote to deny assistance altogether — just like they do with their evidence-less cries about other welfare abuse.

They'd rather a poor child struggle to learn with an aching belly than allow even one "undeserving" parent to receive a single red cent.

Secondly, it's stupid.

Tons of studies have shown that well-fed kids are well-performing kids. Students with adequate nutrition throughout the day score better on tests, show more interest in learning, are less stressed, and generally behave better. It's also been shown that these kids become higher-functioning adults too — they earn more, they're healthier, they're happier, and they commit fewer crimes.

It's the stupid and evil Conservative policy wombo combo! *air horns*

But Conservatives have illustrated time and again how little they care for the long term, and do not concern themselves with improving the future of our population.

They vote to give affluent children as much advantage as possible, and to keep the poor struggling as much as possible. Capitalism demands a steady supply of uneducated wage-slaves, and Conservatives can gladly deliver that order.

We need to feed the damn children. Breakfast, lunch, and maybe even a snack! Every single school needs access to high-quality food and the staff and equipment to prepare it.

Every single school.

We have the resources to make it happen, despite whatever twisted lies Conservative pundits tell.

If this country wants to remain a global superpower, it must invest in the children. Which unambiguously includes feeding them.

SEX EDUCATION

The Conservative playbook here is to refrain from teaching anything related to the consequences of sex at all, and to tell a school full of helplessly horny teenagers to just stop being helplessly horny teenagers.

It's a bold strategy that literally never pays out.

It's also a theocratic bubble of ignorance and hypocrisy.

They preach abstinence-focused education and argue that teaching about sex will only inspire the act, regardless of the what the evidence shows.

EDUCATION

They say sex education is not age-appropriate discussion but then allow child marriages and pressure assaulted children to give birth and raise unwanted children.

They say parents should decide how to teach these things to their kids and deny the children an equal voice in what they learn.

And then we get to the bigots and extremists that want to deny the existence of the LGBTQ+ community. They worry that teaching about that side of sex will morph their kid's entire identity.

They'll say it's a slippery slope — to go from teaching about accepting homosexuals and trans kids to welcoming pedophiles with open arms.

They sure seem suspiciously preoccupied with the rights of pedophiles when things like this come up. Yes they do.

Conservatives, in their stunning ignorance about the realities of life and the fundamentals of consent, just cannot comprehend or appreciate the importance of sex education.

If Conservatives actually gave a shit about protecting our children, like they so heatedly claim, then they'd welcome instructing kids about this core part of life to ensure that they make good choices. Instead, Conservatives worry about government overreach, attack the "alphabet mafia agenda", and stick their heads in the sand.

These children *will* grow up. They *will* have sex. They *will* have varied experiences. Denying that reality is demonstrably foolish.

Children need *medically accurate* knowledge about safe sex and the consequences of unprotected sex.

Children need to be taught about personal boundaries and the fundamentals of consent.

Children need to be shown that consensual love is a very human thing that comes in many forms.

These are principal steps in becoming a well-integrated, empathetic member of society.

We should also mandate comprehensive sex education on a federal level. Parents certainly deserve a choice, but not while depriving that same choice from the kids.

PREPARING KIDS FOR THE REAL WORLD

This is another personal soapbox topic, admittedly. But it ties to criticizing Conservative policy because they're the party of budget cuts and howling about federal curriculum mandates.

As evidenced in the section above, I place great value in equipping schools to adequately prepare kids for the real world. Given that, I want to bring back what is essentially a home economics class like we used to have, but even more involved, and federally mandate it.

Kids need to learn how to budget and do personal finances. They need to understand credit cards and loans and taxes and the fundamentals of managing money. The more they learn about financial principles, the better consumers they can be. We can build their foundation for making wiser decisions about their fiscal future.

Kids need to learn about cooking and nutrition. Some schools do have a health class that goes over some nutrition concepts, but I'd want to mandate that *and* show kids some basics of cooking for yourself. It's not that hard to follow directions and make meals. I think teaching kids to cook and to be mindful of nutrition can have a lasting impact on their health and well-being.

Kids need to learn home improvement skills. I'm not talking about putting up drywall or something that challenging, but doing simple repairs, understanding the infrastructure of a home, and knowing how to handle emergencies as they arise. Teaching them how to fix nail holes or clean out a drain is not going to bankrupt the handyman industry. But it might give kids the confidence to do projects on their own and feel more comfortable when something happens.

Kids need to learn about navigating information on the internet. They need to know about bias and how to spot it. They need to have some knowledge of statistics and the manipulation of numbers. They need to be able to sus out scams and other marketing tricks to avoid being exploited. This will promote the development of critical thinking skills in a relatable way.

Finally, I want to give kids more opportunities to figure out their passions in life and their options for continued education. I want some kind of career exploration course that helps kids really narrow down what they could realistically pursue for college or a trade.

Get them exposed to a variety of different careers — let them tinker with engines, or code a simple app, or work on plumbing, or make a circuit, or draft a building design, or whatever they may be curious about. Let them try out dozens of things to find what sticks out to them!

Schools get so focused on prepping for standardized tests that you find all these kids, myself included, unsure about what they should *do* with their life. We need a stronger emphasis on lighting their way.

These young adults get pushed off to college because so many jobs require degrees. They pick a major that they think will fit, take on loads of debt, and then find out they aren't that passionate about what they chose because they weren't exposed to it before it was too late.

They can't afford to change disciplines or stay in school, so they suck it up and graduate with a degree they never use, and Conservatives just sit back and judge them for their mistake instead of looking to correct how it happened.

Conservatives will probably argue that none of this should be mandated by the government and the parents should just do better at home to prepare their kids for life.

To a degree they are right, but not all kids have parents with the time or skills necessary to teach their children all of these things. It's likely that *their* parents did fuck-all to teach them this stuff either.

It also doesn't make these skills any less essential for ensuring our children have the most future potential that we can offer.

If school is meant to teach kids the skills and subjects essential to becoming bright, productive members of society, then it needs to do more to prime them for reality and to guide them on a path that fits.

STUDENT LOANS

Boomer parents, many of whom had no degree, practically shoved their kids onto the campus streets and forced them to get a bachelor's, no matter the cost. They drilled into these teenagers' heads how valuable college was and how much a degree would serve in life. They pressured their children to take on insultingly high-interest student loans with the promise of abundant job opportunities and a prosperous future.

Then they schemed.

They required applicants for even the most menial jobs to have a bachelor's degree. They perpetuated a system that kept wages low and their children buried in debt long after graduation.

They maximized personal profits by shifting as much manufacturing as they could to countries with cheaper labor. They caused multiple economic downturns and recessions through deregulation and short-sighted policy, which limited job availability for entry-level work.

EDUCATION

They bought up all the property and inflated the cost of living to keep graduates tethered to rentals. They refused to retire or promote younger talent, deriding their lack of experience.

They seized their inheritance and transformed the tax code to further strengthen their financial security while their offspring drowned.

And then they had the fucking gall to mock the students for getting "frivolous" degrees, to chide the children for taking on loans, and to vote for politicians who devalue education and block any attempts to give those students financial respite.

They built this broken system, lectured us to use it, and then punished us for doing so. The cost is somehow our mistake.

Conservatives love to go on furious tirades about the abuses of executive power when a Democrat tries to help everyday Americans. I know my dad was *raging* when Biden tried to forgive a portion of student loans for millions of borrowers and provide some modicum of relief— including for me, his own child.

Oh but when a Republican wants to ignore court orders or dismantle whole departments without Congressional approval or illegally fire government employees or anything else their idiot king decrees, then suddenly executive overreach is no longer a concern.

They do that infuriating, hypocritical shit all the time, don't they?

Countries that actually care about educating their population have manageable college tuition costs or it's simply free.

These smarter nations see higher education as a public good and it's paid for through taxes! What a novel freaking idea!

In the countries that still need student loans, they have better repayment pathways, they get automatic forgiveness after some set time, *and* they either pay zero percent interest or rates get tied to inflation.

Meanwhile here in the mighty U.S. of A. we decided that our students not only needed to go into crippling debt, but the interest rates on their attempts at becoming more educated members of society should be higher than some mortgages and car loans!

Our government decided they wanted to *make some fuckin' money* off of its students!

Oh no, but our government can't manage all that alone! So let's bring in fucking private business loan shark scum to manage everything! These are government-backed loans managed by businesses that care about nothing but profits.

Boy do I *love* the clang of lobbying cash falling into those political campaign buckets!

What could go wrong? Colleges got a free pass to broaden their acceptance criteria, let more and more students in, and raise tuition to the moon while the politicians and business leaders created an ecosystem where a degree is worth less and less and less.

The textbook industry saw the unchecked opportunity to bleed as much money from the influx of students as possible and adopted nonsensical, ravenous business practices.

And property management and private equity firms swooped in to buy all the homes and apartments in college towns so they could keep students suffocated by rent. Their student loans will cover it!

Now student loan debt represents a whopping 10% of all consumer debt, to the tune of nearly $2 *TRILLION*. That's more than all the credit card debt! It's a negative feedback loop disaster and Conservatives want neither to fix it nor to help those already hurt by it.

Higher learning should be a cherished tool for the successful future of a nation. College should be *free* for all who want it.

We can subsidize trade schools too to ensure that we have a well-rounded, skilled workforce.

We can also regulate the insatiable greed of the textbook industry to limit the additional costs of schooling. And I already talked about private equity gobbling up homes in the Capitalism section.

Other advanced countries do this stuff. It's the only way we are going to compete on a global scale.

Maybe some of the silver spoon Ivy League Conservative graduates writing their policies need another elementary economics lesson.

GUN CONTROL

Pretty twisted to put this in the Education section, huh? Well maybe if my niece wasn't making light-hearted jokes about their latest school-shooting drill, I wouldn't feel like it belonged.

Look, even I own a couple of guns myself. I am Texan after all. But I still don't know lot about this topic.

What I *do* know is that Conservative groups accept an incredible amount of lobbying money from the NRA and other relevant special interest groups that make a fortune through gun sales.

I know that Conservative groups have persistently blocked federal efforts at even just *researching* gun violence.

I know that most Conservatives are antagonistic to any model of gun regulation regardless of how many horrors occur.

I know that the U.S. stands alone in its school shooting epidemic and I know that there are policy reasons for it.

And with every new tragedy, there's always a wave of soulless right-wingers that cling to their gun cabinets tighter than the corpses of their bullet-pocked children.

It's heartbreaking that school shootings are as commonplace as any other crimes on the news. We're desensitized.

Schools are supposed to be bastions of learning where kids can feel safe, be sociable, and grow up. Getting gunned down in the hallway between periods should be the last thing on anyone's mind.

But that's not our reality, and Conservatives continued resistance to meaningful change in our gun control laws is to blame. They'd rather get teachers enrolled in gun handling courses — without paying them for the added risk — than pass common sense gun legislation.

Conservatives historically only worry about gun control when minorities start open carrying.

Otherwise, they will point the finger at mental health or poverty or other socioeconomic factors, but then do *nothing* to solve those failings either. Most of their policies dramatically exacerbate those failings!

They give thoughts and prayers instead of laws and action because quelling the catastrophe requires *real* legislation and reform.

They just gobble up NRA cash and kick the can down the road to when the next school shooting sparks this debate again.

"Oh, this tragedy is not the time for politics."

Yes it fucking is! It's exactly the time to *do* something!

Poverty-fighting reform? Funding for mental health professionals? Increased school security? Better-trained police and resource officers? Gun laws?

Bueller?

🛠 HOW WE COULD FIX IT 🛠

Aside from all the various things about poverty and healthcare I've talked about in other sections of this babbling book, the answer is very obviously gun regulation.

That said, I don't know enough about gun laws to have an educated gun regulation-based solution for this. There are a ton of outlines floating around out there — universal background checks, extended waiting periods between buying and receiving a gun, red flag laws that try to keep high-risk people away from guns, safe-storage laws, mandatory free gun safety training courses for new owners, banning various gun attachments, banning specific types of guns, and more.

There is *some* combination of these answers that makes sense and would offer a glimmer of hope that our mass gun violence problems will ease over time.

There is *some* compromise that will appease both the responsible gun nuts *and* the more radical Progressives looking for total bans.

Nah never mind, let's just keep selling bullet-resistant backpacks.

CLOSING RANT

I didn't have the "How We Could Fix It" blurbs in most of these sections because the answer is really simply "put more damn money into education" and I'd get more repetitive than I already am.

Tax the fucking rich, am I right?

The point is that Conservatives have advocated terrible anti-education policies written by deeply anti-poor politicians voted for by woefully anti-intellectual supporters.

It's decades of defunding schools, attacking educators, and perpetuating the cycle of poverty and ignorance.

So many amazing teachers get burned out after just a few years because the pay sucks, the admin sucks, and they feel grossly underappreciated.

Kids sit at their desks with their stomachs growling louder than the lesson because they weren't given food.

Kids are told to ignore the changes to their body and stifle their feelings as a substitute for real discussions about sex and identity.

And if they make it safely through school without bullet wounds, kids are shuffled from high school to college without a firm grasp on their passions and purpose, stepping into their adulthood journey saddled with debilitating debt by a generation that kicked the ladder down.

Our kids deserve better.

THE
ENVIRONMENT

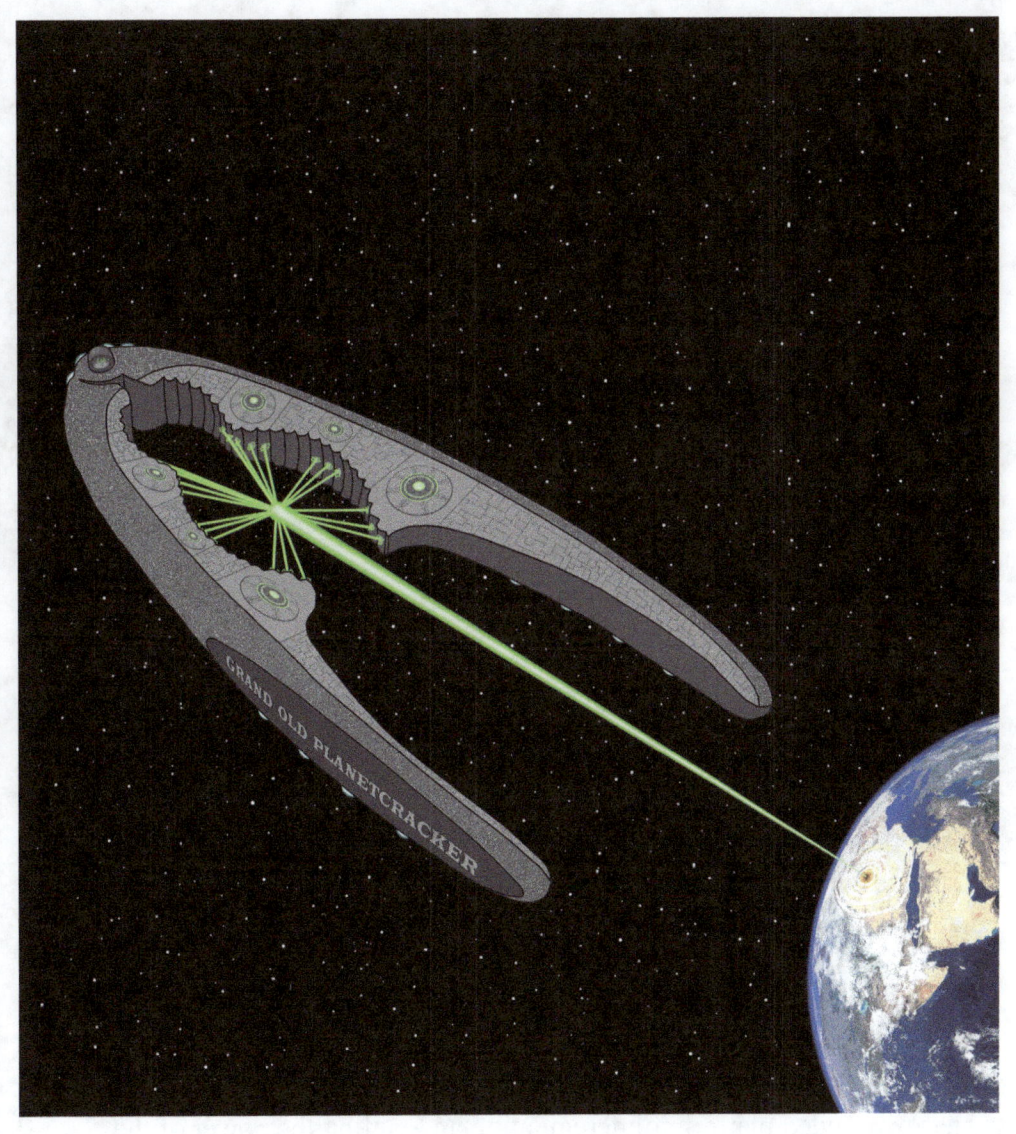

THE ENVIRONMENT

Conservatives live here too, right? They breathe the air? They drink the water? They experience natural disasters? They intend to live on this planet for a while? They have families and children? All of the above?

Okay, I'm just checking because they sure don't vote like they give a shit about the longevity of this blue ball we call home. They *really* seem to care about money and identity politics more than making our home environment as pleasant and safe as possible.

They weren't always like that, either.

Only in the past three or four decades have Republicans shifted to their culture war fear-and hate-mongering strategy and decided that climate change was an alarmist Liberal hoax.

Hell, Nixon created the Environmental Protection Agency! My state has this famous macho anti-littering campaign, "Don't Mess With Texas". George H. W. Bush signed the Clean Air Act! There used to be at least some bipartisan consensus that the planet deserved some love and that the climate was changing for the worse.

And then the oil industry, who *undeniably* knew the realities of climate change even back in the 1970s, decided to do the business-typical thing and lie about it while focusing on short-term profits.

They buried evidence, ran disinformation campaigns, and persistently lobbied Republicans to push out a message of climate change denial.

Now Republicans, with corporate cash in hand, stand firm on their narrowminded platform of deregulation and gutting the power of the EPA every chance they can.

THE ENVIRONMENT

They fiercely defend the "free" market and the God-given right of the fossil fuel industry to siphon every drop of valued resource from our planet without a single fuck to give about the environment. They withdraw us from global conservation agreements and ask their base to viciously smear prominent environmental activists.

Democrats come in and push various pro-Earth policies around that take time to manifest results. Then Republicans regain command and block everything or reverse course, undoing all the progress and sending us back on our destructive path.

This idiotic cycle will just keep going until the west is in flames and the east is submerged.

They all shifted accountability to the individual consumer. The handful of global companies responsible for over 70% of the pollutants and waste concocted the narrative that it's *our* fault and *our* responsibility to be better stewards.

Never mind all the negative externalities of capitalism!

Never mind the hundreds of millions of gallons of spilled oil!

Never mind the billions of tons worth of single-use plastics!

Never mind the countless chemical scandals and coverups!

Never mind the almond farms and golf courses during droughts!

Never mind the blinding ads of Times Square during heat waves!

Never mind the fracking-induced earthquakes!

Never mind the private jets and luxurious yachts!

Only *you*, lowly peon, can save the planet.

Here's a paper straw.

CLIMATE CHANGE

I'm curious how many "once in a lifetime" weather events need to happen every miserable year for Conservatives to accept that the climate is changing and we need to do something?

I know my dad thinks climate change is Liberal propaganda. He'll get red in the face while regurgitating the lies Fox fed him, ardently defending the human impact on our planet's ensuing fever as negligible.

They are the type of people that will wait until it's too late to see reason. Then all the Progressives will peek out of their new mountainside tunnel-homes and say, "We tried to warn you!" and the Conservatives will snap back that we didn't try hard enough or that we're still wrong.

They will probably never, ever take responsibility for their role in what's to come if we do nothing.

Even more frustrating — If Progressives ever do take the majority and are allowed to push lasting, impactful climate policies forward and things *do* get better for Earth, future Conservatives will just point and laugh and say, "See? There was nothing to worry about, snowflakes!"

They'll then slither back into their cozy bed of pure survivorship bias, blissful in the confidence that they owned the Libs.

Conservatives behave like belligerent, rebellious brats constantly battling the will of the adults that know what's best. They'll do shit like throw snowballs on the Senate floor and say it's all fake.

They can't be this stupid, right? I mean I don't think many of the leaders *are* this stupid...well...not *all* of them.

They just prefer to take in gobs of fossil fuel money and live comfortably in the present because they know they'll be dead before their inaction matters.

They don't give a rat's ass about their base! They'll vote to slash FEMA funding right as the next hypercane crashes against Florida!

And now we've (again) withdrawn from the Paris Agreement, the global pact to reduce emissions.

Trump openly calls climate change a hoax and rallies his cult to do the same. He's severed funding for disaster relief and climate research. He's deleted climate information from government websites. He even tried to create a panel of corrupt denialist scientists to stroke his ego and confirm his base's suspicions.

It's a scorched earth campaign in a figurative and literal sense.

It's overblown! It's the Liberal agenda! It's dirty socialism!

Fuck you, Greta! Drill, baby, drill!

If we can't even get them to decide that it's happening at all, there's no shot that they'll ever join in actually doing something about climate change. Their prevailing strategy is to just close down and cut funding for all the groups that research this stuff.

Hey the reported cases of Covid will go down if you just stop testing for it! Problem solved! Same energy.

THE EPA AND REGULATIONS

Trump's first term saw the most pointed and hostile assault on climate science in modern U.S. history.

He rolled back over a hundred EPA regulations and various environmental protection policies. And the Conservatives cheered as the wicked Liberal plan to heal and protect our planet was thwarted.

He repealed the policies that limited carbon and mercury emissions from power plants.

He lifted requirements for oil and gas companies to monitor and repair methane leaks.

He rescinded fracking rules that required the disclosure of chemicals used in the process.

He gutted habitat protections for endangered wildlife at risk of extinction from climate change.

He reduced the land area of various federal monuments to allow them to be developed by businesses.

He ended restrictions on offshore drilling and fossil fuel exploration in the Arctic and Atlantic Oceans.

He overhauled the NEPA to severely limit the environmental reviews for infrastructure projects, including drilling and pipelines.

He dismantled offshore drilling safety regulations that protect workers and even save their lives.

He limited regulations on the disposal of coal combustion residuals.

He weakened fuel efficiency and emissions standards for automobiles.

He redefined the Clean Water Rule to exclude many wetlands and streams from protection.

He rejected a ban on pesticides scientifically linked to developmental issues in children.

He ceased payments to the Green Climate Fund, which aimed to help low-income countries reduce emissions.

He did all of this and much more, all in the name of climate-change denial and "free" market capitalism.

THE ENVIRONMENT

If a past Democrat had tried to do something good for the environment and the future of this country, Trump spitefully repealed it.

And that's just his first term!

We're mere months into his second and he's already enacted the same regressive, retaliatory policies. He's gotten worse. He has more power now than ever before and Conservatives are thrilled to see it.

Now they're attacking the Energy Star program, which has saved Americans hundreds of billions of dollars in energy costs and lowered greenhouse gas emissions.

They're carving out federal land to be sold to the highest bidder.

They're canceling scores of green energy projects.

They're crippling environmental justice initiatives.

They're withholding FEMA funding and telling states to manage disasters themselves.

They're even decimating NOAA, which is an enormously critical agency for monitoring weather and ocean patterns, forecast modelling, and protecting maritime industries and trade. They want to fucking privatize it!

Conservative groups have shown they do not care how many people die from poisoned water, or polluted air, or natural disasters.

They do not care how many kids go hungry.

They do not care how many species are driven to extinction.

They do not care how many times history warns against deregulation.

They do not care about single goddamn thing except making money. Right now. In this moment. The future is someone else's problem.

They would crack the core of the planet just to claim the riches inside.

THE GREEN NEW DEAL

This might as well be my "How We Could Fix It" header since I heavily support everything in the vision of the Green New Deal.

It is exactly the sort of far-reaching, all-encompassing framework that will be vital to bringing meaningful, positive changes to the future of our country, and even the world.

The plan, introduced by someone I hope stays true to their convictions and can be our president someday, is supposed to be the Progressive solution to both climate change and many socioeconomic injustices in this nation.

It's an homage to FDR's New Deal that clawed us out of the Great Depression. You know, the progressive policies that brought America to an age that Conservatives now revere as the "good ol' days" and "when we were great."

The Green New deal has an abundance of excellent ideas, including:

- Reaching net-zero emissions across all sectors of industry — including power, agriculture, infrastructure, manufacturing, and transportation.

- Transitioning our entire country to 100% clean, renewable energy sources including solar, wind, geothermal, and hydroelectric power.

- Modernizing and adapting our power grid to reliably use these new energy sources.

- Updating every single building in the country to be both energy and water-efficient without sacrificing comfort.

- Federally mandating the human right to clean air, clean water, and healthy food.

- Overhauling our transportation system to promote public transit, electric vehicles, and high-speed rails.

- Investing more resources into sustainable agriculture through soil health improvements, efficient land use, and reforming livestock and farming practices.

The plan also has a number of social and economic goals, many of which I've ranted about in other sections of this petty book.

The Green New Deal looks to guarantee livable wages, benefits, and retirement to anyone that wants a job.

It wants to enshrine the right to top-quality healthcare, affordable housing, and all levels of education.

It will prioritize populations that are most disproportionally impacted by environmental and socioeconomic inequalities.

And it will employ the mechanisms required for tight and transparent partnerships between local communities, labor unions, civil rights groups, climate experts, and the government itself.

And it's not like it just forgot about the oil and gas industry. There is a plan to train fossil fuel workers and transition them to work in this new energy landscape. It would shift millions of jobs to these Green projects and create millions more.

The return on investment would be immense, and it would pay dividends long into a future that maintains the vision. It needs work and fine-tuning, but it's a damn good plan.

So, unsurprisingly, Conservatives on all sides have attacked it relentlessly. It's radical socialism! It's government overreach! It's too expensive! Blah blah blah. Same shit, different section.

These people cannot think beyond the next four years. They just sit on their hands and let everything go to hell because they plainly do not care about the future. Why should they care? They'll be dead!

Supreme selfishness is a core tenant of their philosophy, and this is a deeply empathetic plan!

And let's reflect on how idiotic the fossil fuel execs have been all this time. These obscenely wealthy oil and gas leaders saw the writing on the wall half a century ago. They possessed and suppressed their own data on the truth of the climate crisis.

They could have said, "You know what? We're in trouble, so I'm gonna lead the charge and have a big fuckin' oligopoly on green energy. We'll invest in solar panels and wind turbines and geothermal plants and dams and any other renewables we can get our grubby hands on. They're all cheaper, safer, and cleaner in the long run. The Conservatives leaders I pay will love seeing the stock price fly, and the Progressives will finally stop whining about everything I do!"

They could have invested their *tens of trillions* of net profits from the past several decades into gaining full dominion over the Green industry.

But no. The return on investment would take too long. The upfront cost was unacceptable. It's cheaper to keep buying politicians and sucking the Earth dry than to evolve into something better for everyone. That's par for our billionaire overlords.

We're fucked if we don't do something akin to the Green New Deal.

People my age may not feel it. My children may not feel it. But I guarantee that some generation in the near future will bear the disastrous consequences of Conservative inaction. *Someone* is fucked.

It cannot always and forever be Progressives that possess all the long-term critical thought. It's exhausting. And depressing.

166

<u>CLOSING RANT</u>

The Conservative conquest against regulation and the checks on "free" market capitalism will be the death of this country if not this world. They do not learn from history. They do not learn from science. They don't even learn from economics.

It does no good to hope that Conservatives suffer from the outcomes of their heinous, self-centered actions.

I live here too. I want kids. I want my family to have a happy and healthy future. We are all going to be affected by this inevitable environmental reckoning.

We need to take drastic action. We need bold plans. We need strong, Progressive leadership.

And if Conservatives can't even agree that this planet, our home, needs protecting, then I guess we'll have to drag them kicking and screaming, like the petulant children they are, into a better future.

BIGOTRY

BIGOTRY

One of the most defining characteristics of right-wing Conservative movements is their impressively consistent ability to defend and partake in horribly bigoted practices throughout all of history.

Whether it's warring for the right to own human beings as property or blaming immigrants, non-Christians, or rainbow communities for society's problems, you can bet Conservatives will find a way to never take personal responsibility for the evils their policies condone.

The "party of Lincoln", folks. You know, unless you've read a book.

There's always some group to demonize. According to their narrative, it's the minorities — Black Americans, immigrants, anti-capitalists, the LGBTQ+ community, or non-Christians — who cause all the messes and light all the fires and everything wrong with the U.S. can be attributed to their influence.

Just ignore the fact that straight white Christian men have held control over the nation and the bulk of its riches since forever, and that minorities still possess noticeably limited political and corporate representation even today. That does not help their argument!

Doesn't matter, you can bet your ass that Republicans will gerrymander the district maps to guarantee these marginalized groups get only a muffled voice. The Supreme Court said they could!

Remember, some Conservatives believe the Civil Rights Act was a mistake that ushered in the era of DEI bureaucracy, that white privilege is a myth, and that the Great Replacement Theory is upon us.

It's like they sit around a conference room at the Murdoch mansion and talk about which group they want to focus on this cycle and how best to attack them. Looks like the 2025 Wheel of Outrage landed on trans people and Hispanics! We'll spin it again in 2026!

Their fear of the "other" is quite the gem of hypocrisy because often they too descend from one of those "others" they disparage. Many white Americans came from a family of immigrants seeking a better life or fleeing religious persecution. Just like my dad's family. Most of us would try to flee unsafe, violent situations like war or cartels.

Conservatives are starved of both historical awareness and human empathy. They forget the path that brought them here, and they're apathetic to the similar hardships others face today.

And in the case of racial, sexual, religious, or some other identity differences, Conservative movements have consistently failed to fully accept anyone who doesn't fit their narrow vision of what a person "should" be.

If you're a white, straight, Christian, American-born male — like Jesus was, of course — then you're on the "good list". You lose points for straying from any of those categories. You get a few bonus points for being Conservative, and the maximum bonus points if you're rich.

Ultimately it comes down to Conservative ideology harshly judging people for how they are born instead of by the merits of their work ethic, societal contribution, and character. Like they project onto DEI.

I realize how hypocritical I sound given that this whole mouthy book enthusiastically generalizes Conservatives and their worldview, but I did say "societal contribution" and "character".

I've ranted a lot already on the harmful global impact of Conservative policy, and if someone's value system involves things like robbing schoolchildren of lunch money or denying innocent humans equal rights, then they have shit character too. Shrug.

Judge people for things they *can* control, not things they can't.

DIVERSITY, EQUITY, AND INCLUSION

Conservative pundits really get off on crafting little buzzwords or maliciously commandeering existing phrases to use as dog whistles, signaling all the like-minded bigots into action.

"Welfare queens", "political correctness", "safe spaces", "critical race theory", etc. — There has been an endless onslaught of these phrases tossed around throughout U.S. history. When I was growing up it was "affirmative action" that my dad always complained about.

Today it's "DEI" and all things "Woke".

Half the time the Conservative media and politicians can't even define these things when you ask them. They just know the soundbites and how they trigger the anger in their audience.

But it's all the same strategy — a call for tribalism and scapegoating. It's their endless culture war, and today it's the "woke mind virus" threatening their heritage! You know, the heritage of literal traitors to the country that took up arms against their countrymen to protect *slavery*.

Can't find a job? Must be cuz companies only do *DEI* hires!

Your kid failed math? Must be cuz the teacher did *CRT!*

Your business failed? Must be cuz you didn't sell that *WOKE* shit!

Here is a list of fun things I have literally seen or heard Conservatives blame DEI and "Woke" for:

- Air traffic control or pilot errors
- Infrastructure failures
- Finance and cybersecurity breaches
- Waning medical, STEM, and general education standards
- Declining entertainment quality

- Stock market underperformance
- Banking collapses
- Government inefficiency
- Decreasing military discipline and readiness
- Rising labor incompetence
- Lapsing police hiring standards

Doubtless the list could get so much longer and more ridiculous, but you get the idea.

Conservative voices excel at either wildly misattributing the cause of real problems or inventing non-existent problems to feed the outrage.

"DEI in the Miltary" (sic) is not a real concern. There isn't a shred of credible evidence that so-called "DEI units" perform worse than a group comprised of only straight white soldiers. DEI policies don't waive the physical or technical standards required to serve. It's just utterly asinine and disingenuous to suggest otherwise.

Veteran-loving Conservatives also must've forgotten that the U.S. military is volunteer-based, and alienating potential recruits through bigotry isn't a winning strategy for bolstering the ranks.

DEI doesn't cause companies to fail. Biden's term saw a significant market recovery post-Covid and many companies hitting all-time highs in the stock market. Conservative pundits just cherry-picked random companies that maybe had an unimpressive earnings call or they saw a bad Disney movie and screeched, "Must be all the women and minorities in charge!" "Go WOKE, Go BROKE!"

Meanwhile, loads of companies that embrace diversity, equity, and inclusion are thriving.

DEI is not the cause of waning education standards. U.S. education constantly gets budget cuts, teachers' salary is still the butt of a bad joke, poverty is rampant, standardized tests are prioritized over critical thought, and children are left hungry because Conservatives refuse to fund school meals.

But nah it's totally because we hire too many minority teachers, not the decades of Conservative efforts to devalue public education.

This nonsense needs to be called out for what it is — racism, genderism, ableism, heterosexism, nativism, classism, and every other –ism rooted in the bigotry lexicon.

Deep breath now. We have a Conservative-run, proto-fascist government that's gone around deleting all mentions of DEI, firing workers that do any job even tangentially related to DEI, firing workers they think were only hired for DEI, halting all funding for any research or for any institution that has anything to do with DEI or supports DEI initiatives, rewriting the histories of civil servants and distinguished military that they see as unworthy DEI stories, and every manner of other horrific, misguided erasures of the importance of diversity, equity, and inclusion.

These are some of the very first things they did when they won in 2025!

They want to erase all acknowledgment of the abundant privileges that straight white men have enjoyed for centuries.

They refuse to admit that these minorities and marginalized groups have never been on a fair playing field. Hence the marginalized.

The deck has been so strongly stacked against them in so many ways by the relentless systemic bullshit and discriminatory practices scattered throughout our history: Slavery, Jim Crow laws, forced sterilizations, redlining, mass deportations, the Lavender Scare, immigrant internment camps, exclusion policies, insurance denial, job denial, marriage denial, healthcare denial, human rights denial…

Conservative voices remain incapable of admitting the necessity of programs like Affirmative Action, Equal Opportunity Employment, and

DEI — These programs that are simply trying to give those groups the same level of opportunity that the privileged class has enjoyed for time immemorial. White privilege unequivocally exists.

Something really snapped in this country's collective consciousness when a charismatic black man was elected president. Thanks, Obama.

✂ HOW WE COULD FIX IT ✂

This country — really, this world — has always been riddled with bigots. It can't be fixed but with time and newer generations raised with a sense of acceptance and empathy.

It *has* improved some over time, though with every Conservative election victory the progress line dips. All the bigots come out of the woodwork and share their hateful voices loud and proud, emboldened by their leaders pushing hateful, exclusionist policies forward.

Empowering the worst racists our country has to offer has a way of making other racists feel like their voice deserves a volume level higher than mute.

Being generally kind to everyone and having an understanding that different cultures and backgrounds exist is considered "woke" now. Saying "everyone is welcome" in your classroom makes you a radical leftist worthy of censorship and expulsion.

Despite all that, the equality progress line technically *is* trending upwards if you zoom out on the chart.

We need to support the trend by reinstating as many of these DEI-like programs as we can because the evidence shows that they have a plethora of benefits, contrary to Conservative pundit hatemongering.

I don't think all the –isms will ever really die out, but the fewer right-wing extremists there are in charge, the less power their toxic, malevolent messages carry.

So I'll do my part to fix it by voting for Progressives and raising my children to be empathetic. Empathetic, but with no tolerance for Conservative-flavored hate.

<u>MERITOCRACY</u>

I wanted to rant about this because it's one of the most common words that Conservatives use to justify their prejudice against all things DEI.

It's the opinion that there are people being elevated to positions of leadership and success that do not deserve it on their own merits. They got there through a skin tone and sexuality filter that tosses out qualified straight white male candidates in favor of unqualified losers with a particular skin tone, set of genitals, or sexual preference.

Never mind the unapologetic advertisement of their bigotry in denying the possibility that these minorities could *actually* be qualified, do they really think that the top businesses are hiring swarms of inept diversity drones to make all the important decisions and risking their precious shareholder value for the sake of DEI?

Do they really think that marketers wouldn't immediately abandon diversity-related strategies if they were losing influence or money?

Do they really think that the most elite schools would want their dropout rates to skyrocket from a huge influx of unfit students?

There are no federal laws mandating a hiring quota for diverse candidates. Private employers and institutions can talk all they want about their diversity goals, but they are not mandated to actually *do* shit.

Lots of businesses have blind hiring policies in place to safeguard an unbiased process. Countless schools have been historically deficient at accepting minorities and they alter their guidelines to see that potentially splendid students aren't excluded based on socioeconomic injustices or identity culture war drivel.

All this Conservative wailing about meritocracy is just another dog whistle in their heavy whistle bag.

And go figure, they are also colossal hypocrites here too. You want to talk about getting into positions of power based on merit alone? Holy crap look at the people you elect!

The Conservatives that get nominated to the highest offices in the country are some of the most unqualified, regulatory-captured disasters they could have possibly chosen!

- A Fox-news talking head with flimsy military experience to be the Secretary of Defense.

- A retired neurosurgeon as the Secretary of Housing and Urban Development whose only qualifications for the job were "used to live in public housing".

- A dude with a pile of ethics violations and multiple frivolous lawsuits targeting the EPA chosen to be its Administrator, and then a goddamn coal lobbyist to direct the EPA after.

- A billionaire with deep investments in the student loan industry and who never set foot in a public school to serve as the Secretary of Education.

- Another billionaire with an incredibly shady business past to be the Secretary of Commerce.

- Yet another fucking billionaire whose only experience is pro wrestling to handle the Small Business Administration.

- A known fraudster that wasn't even aware of what Secretary of Energy did, yet still got the job.
- Trump's completely clueless, corrupt children and other family and friends to serve as official advisors to the highest office.
- Trump himself.

I mean the list really could go on and on.

Are Democrats perfect here? Of course not. But they aren't the ones yelling about the death of merit-based hiring because a few minorities got put in charge.

So maybe Conservatives should shut the fuck up and look their own hiring pool. Or just stfu in general.

🛠 HOW WE COULD FIX IT 🛠

Honestly this whole process needs a fresh coat. There are too many unqualified dipshits and walking conflicts-of-interest in charge of our government. I'm not actually sure what the cause is here and how these people get confirmed. Perhaps it's the combination of nepotism, quid pro quo, and outright lying during the confirmation hearings.

We need laws that require certain standards for education and experience. It's maddening to me that a qualifying resume is so focal for the rest of us to get a job, but somehow not for the Cabinet or top advisors. Or the president.

We need more career civil servants running the government, not ghoulish sycophants and depraved billionaires. It's like putting a bunch of rabid foxes in charge of the henhouses.

We need robust ethics laws and investigations that are actually *enforced* to prevent even an inkling of a financial entanglement with these people.

We need to reform the Senate confirmation process to more concretely prove that these people know what the fuck they are doing for the job, mandate the full disclosure of financials and other conflicts before the hearing, and close loopholes that allow these high-ranking positions to be filled too hastily and without enough scrutiny.

And we need to actually hold these people accountable for lying about any of this. They'll get confirmed and then quickly show the world how dishonest they were at the hearing. And yet nothing happens.

Any other government worker that gets caught lying about their conflicts of interest or their qualifications would get fired, fined, barred from continued service, and possibly imprisoned.

Somehow the more important your position, the less that accountability and a solid resume matter. Especially to Republicans.

IMMIGRATION

What a topic. If there was one issue that was always at the forefront of Conservative fearmongering and bigotry, it's immigrants.

All across the world, immigrants are used as political punching bags. They are apparently why there's no jobs. They are apparently why there's no homes. They are apparently why it's so crowded. They are apparently why we have no resources left for citizens.

There's no fault given to the failed systems and tragic events that caused them to flee their country though. Ever.

It's not late-stage capitalism creating rampant poverty. It's not the wicked warmongers of the world using their limited time on this planet to be villainous garbage. It's not the religious fanatics casting out anyone that doesn't believe in the same sky daddy rulebook. No no no, it's the *immigrants* causing problems.

Conservatives show no empathy for these people. Empathy is woke.

They'll sit there in their comfortable recliner with their sagging beer belly and a tray of TV Dinner slop while Fox shrieks about a lawless open border and the looming immigrant hordes.

Their eyes twitch at the light of the flatscreen as an exhausted, desperate mother limps across a border checkpoint, cradling a crying baby in one arm and clutching her confused, soil-dusted children with the other.

The couch warrior chokes down a bite, pops an antacid, then spits out the phrase, "They should just go back where they came from!"

Conservatives must have some strangely high opinions of themselves and how they would handle harsh situations. If their emotional intelligence was capable of wearing an immigrant's shoes, I bet they'd see themselves as some kind of badass saviors.

They'd take their vault of firearms and fight the cartels or the warlords or the oligarchs that stole everything from them! Fuck yeah!

In my opinion, Conservatives are too selfish to care about the hardships of others, too clueless to understand how they support the systems creating the hardships, and too insulated from the effects of their hate and ignorance to change their minds.

Now they cheer at the rallies as the masked cowards of ICE sweep through communities, arresting non-whites without oversight, without warrants, and without due process.

The crime of being brown.

They gleefully piss and shit all over the Constitution and the fundamental rights of all people on this country's soil, regardless of citizenship status, while praying to the orange god they made.

Oh, but Conservatives love to reap the *benefits* of immigration!

They love exploiting a stream of hardened laborers for agriculture and construction that they can hire for scraps. They love the cheap food and other goods filling the shelves of supermarkets. They love the job those undocumented folks did on the deck of their McMansion. They love the cleaning lady that keeps their home spotless.

And they'll gladly deport them all.

Conservatives are always eager to seek judgment on the poor workers, but never the contractors and tech bros that exploit the system. It's never the "job creators" at fault for bringing immigrants over illegally to work for illegally-low wages. No, it's the fault of the poor immigrants for being desperate enough to risk it all.

Conservatives also ignore or forget how pivotal immigrants are to our current labor system.

Americans do not *want* to do the sorts of jobs that these immigrants are doing — the back-breaking, skin-scalding, often thankless labor of building our homes, paving our roads, growing our food, and so much more. They clean places we live and work, they serve as caretakers to our children and elderly, and they offer low-cost services to grease the wheels of commerce.

They do so much for us and our relatively comfortable lives.

These people pay billions in taxes. These people keep costs down. These people are deeply woven into our economic system and are integral to its upkeep and its future.

But Conservatives do not care. They have an intensely xenophobic platform, and immigrants are of the "other".

Their politicians ignore the devastating impact of their own policies, and instead use the ignorance and bigotry of their base to cast blame on this very vulnerable and important group of people.

They'll support mass deportation efforts, suspend Constitutional rights, spread lies about crime rates, and waste billions on walls and enforcement all in the name of protecting us from a group of people we sorely need.

They'll let Gravy Seal racists play military dress-up, hiding their face and brandishing rifles as they march through neighborhoods to sow fear.

They'll patrol a city in unmarked cars before arresting quiet tourists for being suspiciously pigmented.

They'll use poorly doctored photos as proof of gang affiliation and post them throughout their "news" networks.

They'll tear children from their parents without care or a plan to reunite the families with their loved ones.

They'll invade the homes of citizens without warrants, even posing as immigration officials or utilities providers to deceive trusting minorities.

They'll ambush law-abiding migrants at their scheduled immigration appointments and court hearings.

They'll use every fascist tool imaginable to push the narrative that immigrants, illegal or not, are a thorn in this nation's side.

I remember when one of the Midterm elections was coming up, and all the right-wing media could talk about what some migrant caravan making its way towards our border.

My dad was watching intently, I'm sure.

BIGOTRY

The fearmongering was honestly hilarious. This large group of harmless migrants was just going to steamroll right over the border checkpoint and claim citizenship or something. It was all they talked about! The caravan! *spooky caravan noises*

We have such vast military might, yet we are supposed to fear these field hands, roof-layers, and housekeepers.

Well, then the Midterms ended, and all of a sudden that caravan was no longer newsworthy. It either didn't exist anymore or it was such a non-threat that it was dealt with quietly. Typical.

"You guys better elect a Conservative Congress or else this caravan is gonna git ya!"

And their Confederate-traitor-flag-waving base ate up that bait as ravenously as they do anything served on a propaganda platter.

It was just such a wonderful example of Conservative tactics. And though it didn't work that year, it indubitably worked when Drumpf, who comes from a family of immigrants, was elected again in 2024.

This time, Biden's "OPEN BORDER" was the new hot button racist topic. It's wide open, folks!

On Fox, Biden was laughing maniacally as he let droves of illegals skip freely into the country. In the real world, there were record numbers of deportations and removals under his admin. Biden even asked for more money from Congress for border enforcement, and Republicans blocked it because they needed their "OPEN BORDER" scare for votes!

They are always full of shit, but their voters don't know or don't care. Conservatives don't even seem to care if the immigrants are legal or not at this point.

Immigrants are an easy target, and Conservatives keep lots of ammo.

⚒ HOW WE COULD FIX IT ⚒

There are many pathways to making immigration both more efficient and more humane.

For starters, we need some kind of self-governing immigration court that is separated from the Department of Justice.

This independent, unbiased court — removed from all the political grandstanding and bullshit — can take an army of asylum officers, immigration judges, child advocates, and other legal representatives and efficiently streamline the convoluted barrier of a process for getting immigrants legal status under asylum, or work visas, or whatever designation is relevant.

We can cut funding from ICE and give it to organizations that actually care for immigrants and their struggles.

We can replace for-profit detention centers with facilities that humanely house and/or offer case management services for immigrants awaiting counsel or judgment. I talk about my animosity towards for-profit prisons in the Justice section, but these places are just Hell on Earth and often house mostly harmless people.

We can establish reasonable pathways to citizenship for undocumented people that have lived and worked here for years without so much as a speeding ticket. These people deserve citizenship.

We can expand the H-1B and seasonal work visa programs and severely punish organizations that exploit these laborers.

We can improve on our ability to track and care for unaccompanied minors and put an immediate stop to family separation policies.

We can try all of this, but good luck finding a Conservative legislature with enough empathy and economic understanding to pass those laws.

THE LGBTQ+ COMMUNITY

There's a simple question I've asked my dad when talking about things like gay marriage.

"Why do you fucking care?"

Seriously, why do you people give one infinitesimal iota of a fuck what gay people do behind closed doors?

Why are you so hellbent on making sure they can't, with consent, marry whoever they want? Why do you want to be so involved?

Imagine spending your limited time on this rock so laser focused on who other people love or how they identify. What a cringey, pathetic way to go about life.

The same sentiment goes for all the other letters in the "alphabet mafia". It's baffling enough that you have to wonder if the loudest voices come from the most closeted people. They usually do.

My dad's answer to the gay marriage question is some fumbling word salad nonsense about how the Constitution defines marriage. Go figure, the Constitution doesn't define marriage at all, but that won't stop Conservatives like him from having a Fox-implanted opinion about it.

I've got a friend with a rich, lifelong Republican father. The man was staunchly against gay marriage just up until the point where one of his nieces came out as gay. How quickly he tossed out his hateful convictions about marriage because now it affects *him* and his family! The dude later officiated a different gay wedding!

I mean good on him for seeing the light, but this is the classic Conservative move. "Whoops it affects *me* now. Better shake up my whole worldview." Where has your empathy been hiding all this time?

185

This segment isn't really just about marriage, though marriage is emblematic of one of those fundamental rights battles that this community has struggled with for effectively forever.

The LGBTQ+ community is yet another frequent target for Conservative hatred and anti-human rights policies.

Conservatives voted to criminalize their very identity and existence up until 2003.

Conservatives pushed for non-hetero military members to keep their sexuality a secret before that got repealed in 2011.

Conservatives limit or outright ban books and discussions on LGBTQ+ existence in schools.

Conservatives try to prevent same-sex couples from adopting children.

Conservatives celebrate legal exemptions allowing businesses to discriminate against the LGBTQ+ community.

Conservatives fought back against ACA provisions that prohibited LGBTQ+ discrimination for healthcare coverage.

Conservatives support institutions that perform barbaric conversion therapies like trying to electrocute the queer out of someone.

Conservatives tried to federally define marriage as only between a man and a woman before the landmark 2015 decision that legalized gay marriage — which is now being contested by Conservatives *again*.

And lately the focus has been on the transgender community and a relentless assault on all things related to gender identity.

Conservatives have long reviled that community, but their targeted animosity has escalated much in recent years. Their crusade against L, G, and B failed, so they shifted over to TQ+.

They complain about the miniscule number of transgender athletes competing, they clutch their pearls in fear of using gender neutral bathrooms, they protest against innocuous drag shows, and they roll their eyes at gender-identifying email signatures.

Do you think a certain author's boggart would come out of the box as a large, lumbering pronoun?

It's also ironic seeing these right-wing dude-bro alpha-male dangerously insecure types judge the trans community and their gender-affirming care despite themselves guzzling steroids, human growth hormone, unregulated supplements, and various drugs to affirm their own masculinity. I'd feel sorry for their mental health issues if they weren't using their platform to spread hate.

You missed a spot with your eye liner there, JD.

One of the first things Orange Mussolini did was federally define the existence of only two genders. They are barring trans people from serving in the military, enacting birth-assigned gender bathroom laws, and banning gender-affirming care among other vile things.

As I write this, Conservatives have just voted to strip the transgender community of gender-affirming healthcare through Medicaid. They literally removed the 'T' from LGBT-related government content.

When in power, Conservatives do whatever they can to dismantle the human rights of the rainbow communities and attack any institutions or businesses that resist.

They bully and weaken a group that only accounts for a small fraction of the population. They fabricate statistics about trans athletes, concoct bullshit stories about children and their health decisions, and rile up a base that sits undeservedly on a throne of moral superiority they believe their sky daddy built them.

They'd rather shepherd suicide numbers to new heights than address the depravity of their bigotry.

There's definitely a large religious influence in all this — and I get into that in another chapter — but I think that most of their disconnect comes down to their inability to understand the concept of *consent*.

Conservatives can get really confused when you bring up that word. They'd have to check a dictionary if they didn't burn it already.

They are the type of people that can't grasp that a woman's outfit is not an invitation for sex.

They are the type of people that deliberately keep archaic child-marriage laws on the books because they don't understand that children are not mentally capable of true consent.

They are the type of people that want abstinence-only education in schools, instead of living in reality where the rules of consent and safe practices need to be illustrated.

They are the type of people that elect a man infamous for bragging about violating consent.

So they attack gay couples that are consenting to join together for life.

They attack the drag community for consenting to express themselves through fashion and entertainment, and attack the adults consenting to enjoy the show.

They attack kids that undergo years of psychiatric therapy and ultimately consent to gender reassignment.

They attack people for the way they are born, and attack the people that show support for the different way of life.

They do not care about the facts with this community, or any other for that matter. They just need a target for their culture wars.

They can't just *shut the fuck up* and let consenting adults be consenting adults. They can't just let consenting people love who they want, marry who they want, and/or be whatever gender they want.

Their obsession goes so far it's almost suspicious.

Meanwhile the Republican party protects and elects pedophiles while crying to "think of the children".

Maybe Conservatives should turn their disgust inwards.

🛠 HOW WE COULD FIX IT 🛠

We need to refine any federal policies related to civil liberties, including the Civil Rights Act and Title IX, to explicitly include protections for sexual orientation and gender identity. That alone would go pretty far in helping that community combat the deluge of discriminatory state-level laws and practices.

We can ban and criminalize conversion therapy. We can improve access to gender-affirming care, mental health, and psychiatric services (especially to youth). We can implement a robust and inclusive sex education program. And we can protect marriage equality for all consenting partnerships.

I was also horrified to learn that we have shit policies regarding LGBTQ+ refugees seeking asylum and have been known to deport them back to countries that are somehow even worse bigots. That obviously needs to be fixed too.

Seriously, Conservatives. What harm have these people ever brought into your life? I'm not talking about the fallacious anecdotes you hear on Fox. I'm talking about *real* evidence of harm.

These communities aren't hurting others, they aren't hurting themselves, and they unquestionably aren't hurting the potential of our nation.

It is so long past time they get full Constitutional protection.

WOMEN

Dear Conservative women,

Are you okay? What are you doing?

The men in your party do not give one flying fuck about you, your freedoms, your troubles, or your well-being.

You are only a tool for their amusement, a laborer for their homestead, and an incubator for their heirs.

They see you as beneath them in every way — from brains to brawn.

They don't want you making the business decisions.

They don't want you making the government decisions.

They don't want you in positions of authority or in any scenario where the women command more control than the men.

They want to drag you back to the days when you cleaned the house alone, remained perpetually pregnant, and spent your time cooking in the kitchen with your mouth shut while the men made all the money and held all the power.

Maybe some of you are all about that subservient, unequal "trad wife" crap. I wish there was some self-respect, but fine.

That doesn't mean you have the right to push that toxicity onto every other woman.

You spit in the face of every women's rights activist in history.

It was Progressives that gave you the right to vote.

It was Progressives that paved the way for you to open your own bank account and take charge of your finances.

It's Progressives that seek to protect you from harassment and discrimination in the workplace.

It's Progressives fighting to protect no-fault divorce rights.

It's Progressives that will codify your right to choose.

It's Progressives trying to treat you with equality.

It's Progressives that support abuse victims.

And it's Progressives that will get the first female president elected.

Why do you support the party and platforms in direct opposition to those freedoms, values, and dreams?

Guess we'll have to consult the only chart in this sad book.

With concern,

-Radic, the Progressive

🛠 HOW WE COULD FIX IT 🛠

Same way we fix everything in this section I guess — raise better kids.

Teach them the value and impact of women.

Teach them the history of rights-suppression so they know how much effort it took to get here.

Teach them how to be supportive friends and partners.

Teach them about the physiology of women's cycles.

Teach them to speak out when they witness harm and hate.

Teach them about consent, respect, and empathy.

On the policy side —

We could codify Roe v. Wade.

We could expand funds for domestic violence and rape reporting (not just for women).

We could encourage higher-education paths for women (like STEM).

We could open investigations into (and severe penalties for) companies that vary pay based on things like gender.

And we could get religion out of politics (many religions are anti-women, go figure).

Honestly lots of things discussed in this bonfire-bound book would go a long way to empowering women in our world's long history of suppressing their rights and potential.

<u>CLOSING RANT</u>

I sometimes think about what the bigots of the far future will look like.

When normal government policy has finally caught up to the point where Conservative voices no longer have power over any letter of the rainbow communities, when immigrants are again welcomed as the backbone of our country, when misogyny is a remnant of a bygone era, and when all the minorities finally feel like they stand on equal ground...

BIGOTRY

What then will the racists and bigots be shitbags about?

Robot marriage? Holodeck relationships? Maybe we've met some cool aliens by then?

The bigots never fully disappear; they just adapt to the times.

Like I've said, the best way to fix this is to raise better, empathetic children. These views are taught.

Evidence has shown that kids are not generally born as bigots.

It's the shitty parents, the corrupt online influencers, the evil politicians, and the paid-off propagandists who poison our young with the fear and the hatred of anything that looks differently or sounds differently or worships differently.

It'll take many generations and many more societal reforms before "extraterrestrial rights" becomes the next DEI controversy.

By the way, there are roughly 394 personal pronouns in this chapter!

JUSTICE

JUSTICE

"We don't have a justice system, we have a legal system."

Look I'm not a lawyer, and I have no experience with the crazy complex inner workings of the law and how all the gears of justice turn.

All I know is that both our perception *and* the reality of a rotten, biased justice system in this country have alarmingly worsened lately. It doesn't just look bad, it *is* bad.

It has never been more evident that our laws are enforced by a measure of one's wealth before all else.

It has never been more evident that our leaders have eroded any sense of ethical accountability for Congress and the Courts.

It has never been more evident that the police are not obligated to serve and protect the lower class.

It has never been more evident that the Executive's abuses of pardon powers will send us further down the path of textbook authoritarianism.

There are so many different tiers to our system.

Are you rich or poor? Are you famous or nameless? Are you a Republican or a Democrat? Are you white or a person of color?

The law gets applied differently depending on how such questions get answered, as if each crime has some dystopian flow chart attached that can result in different outcomes and penalties.

We are always told that "No one is above the law."

That's the bullshit phrase the rich and powerful use to maintain the illusion of equitable justice so us plebians don't step out of line or push for change. There has been a plethora of examples of criminals being carried above the law in just the past ten years alone.

We literally have a convicted felon as president. It doesn't get any more unbelievably unjust than that.

The entire system needs rebalancing, because the scale is broken and Lady Justice got bribed.

The evidence is overwhelming.

CORPORATE CRIME

Why was barely anyone held accountable for the 2008 financial crisis which caused millions to lose their homes and livelihoods?

Why were there only fines and probation for the scam Wells Fargo pulled opening fake accounts in unsuspecting customers' names?

Why does the Sackler family get to walk free and stay pathologically wealthy despite their role in the opioid crisis?

Why were HSBC execs not criminally charged for actively laundering billions for drug cartels and organized crime?

Why were no GM execs imprisoned for knowingly letting a defect persist and cause the deaths of more than a hundred people?

Why are Boeing execs allowed to mock regulators and withhold safety information while their planes crash and kill passengers?

The list of questions is endless with this type of white-collar crime — where executives are encouraging some kind of unethical, anti-consumer, outright dangerous behavior and nobody goes to prison for it.

Even worse, the companies often get to coast by on a Non-Prosecution Agreement with some monetary penalty that merely puts a fucking dent in the profits they generated while running their scam.

The executives will just resign, wipe their tears with enough severance cash to last multiple lifetimes, and float away on their golden parachute while the company gets to scam on.

It's a putrid form of pay-to-play justice.

These bastards belong behind bars. Instead, they are shielded from liability with tricks like indemnification clauses, which protect these business leaders from legal costs, fines, and other damages if they commit crimes for the job.

Their companies get to pinky-swear that they'll be well-behaved little capitalists and we're all just supposed to look the other way.

They so often evade justice because Conservatives and Republicans love gutting both fraud reporting agencies and whistleblower protections.

They love deregulation and limiting corporate oversight.

They love rampant regulatory capture, appointing pro-businesses judges, and nominating wealthy businessmen to lead government agencies.

Meanwhile you get the more center-right Democrats that publicly claim they want to do better at cracking down on this crime, but then spectacularly fumble the hammer when it's their turn to prosecute the white-collar criminals.

There is an enormous quasi-legal, extrajudicial system in place to protect these elite businesspeople and their enterprises from real accountability and from the cold humility of prison cells.

It's a big club, and we plebs aren't in it.

✖ HOW WE COULD FIX IT ✖

I love how companies *are* people when it comes to political campaign donations, but they *aren't* people when it comes to justice. Perfectly balanced, as all things should be.

We need to actually punish the leaders of companies when they are proven to have intentionally committed crimes, and their sentences need to be proportional to the damage they caused.

We need to end the concept of "too big to fail". The fuck kind of "free" market is that? Bring back the days of shattering both monopolies and the pricing cartels that form when competition is smothered.

Our tax dollars should not be used to bail out these nefarious, scheming, wealthy crooks or to subsidize their monopolistic growth and their desires to price gouge us for basic services.

We need to heavily reevaluate Deferred and Non-Prosecution Agreements to allow for more transparency and a public legal record of misconduct. No more hiding. No more slaps on the wrist.

We need to protect whistleblowers and give better rewards for reporting corporate and government abuses. Guess which party has been threatening the livelihood of whistleblowers?

We need to enhance funding for all the agencies and organizations that are designed to investigate and prosecute white-collar crime. Guess which party has been slashing the resources and personnel for every single one of these groups? Hint: it's the same fascists as above.

We need to ban Non-Disclosure Agreements (NDAs) in cases where the public was negatively impacted. These corporate goblins harmed the public and the public deserve to know how justice was served.

Finally, we need to outlaw indemnification clauses in cases involving fraud or gross misconduct. No more sheltering behind some bylaw or corporate contract.

These executives need to develop the same fear of the law that the poor have always known.

FINES AS PUNISHMENT

This is how a two-tiered justice system is born. Where the rich and poor can commit the same crime yet see dramatically different punishments.

If I get a speeding ticket for $500, that will set me back an amount that actually hurts and I'll be driving like a granny for a while. If some rich asshole gets the same speeding ticket, that $500 is completely meaningless to them and does nothing to deter the behavior.

Now go bigger. If some company gets caught committing fraud, they may get fined some flat penalty per offense and pay a few million dollars, right? That's cool by them — it's just the cost of doing business!

They'll pass those fines along to shareholders or raise prices for consumers to cover that fine and they can move on to the next scam. It's literally built into their operating costs! The fine for breaking the law is just a line on their balance sheet.

Flat fines are not good enough. They are a regressive justice system that puts far more pressure on the poor than the rich. If the *point* of a fine is to be an impactful price for wrongdoing, then it needs to sting for both rich and poor alike.

Corporate fines are the same way. If a company just casually absorbs fines into their criminal business practice budget, then the fines are not doing enough to deter the behavior.

🛠 HOW WE COULD FIX IT 🛠

We need to adopt a progressive punishment system. It needs to be a percentage of net worth, or income, or some measure of wealth so that the poor aren't devastated by that speeding ticket and the rich asshole might think twice about it themselves.

I want to put an end to the days where a company can get some piddly-ass fine for their crimes and scams. These acts affect thousands, even millions of lives!

We need to financially obliterate companies and/or executives that even *try* to pull off these scams. We need to invoke criminal punishments for criminal business leaders and fine the companies by some large percentage over the value that their crimes generated.

If it's determined that a company made $50 million off some price gouging scheme, then they need to get fined $250 million or something. Companies with repeat offenses deserve the death sentence by revoking their charter and barring them from future business here.

Take it out of executive bonuses. Let the workers sue leadership. Install auditing programs to verify that these companies don't just lay off a ton of workers, cut wages, raise prices, or do stock buybacks to cover the cost of their crimes. The fines themselves can be earmarked to help affected victims and workers.

There are well-known ways to encourage businesses and executives to play by the rules, but Congress won't bite the hand that feeds them.

You know, other countries do this stuff. Other countries actually send white-collar criminals to jail and have proportional fines for illegal acts. Their markets still stand. The U.S. just cares about safeguarding businesses and the 1% more than having an equitable justice system.

<u>POLITICAL CORRUPTION</u>

Carter had to give up his peanut farm, y'all.

And yet here we are — with lawmakers throwing emoluments clauses into the wind, shamelessly trading stocks with insider knowledge, and openly embracing the once-quiet corruption cracking every branch of the U.S. government.

This second Trump administration has to be the most blatantly corrupt government in our history, right? I mean it's definitely dethroning the first-place spot earned in his first term.

We've got the dismantling of ethics committees and anti-corruption groups, we've got campaign finance laws being abandoned, we've got dramatic reductions in foreign influence protection programs, we've got the firing of the officials that enforce ethics in Congress...

I mean if I wanted to have a disturbingly corrupt organization, I certainly wouldn't want any of *those* pesky laws and watchdogs around!

That way I could go around committing all sorts of ethics violations like:

- endorsing crypto memecoin scams
- accepting a "palace in the sky" from the Saudis
- posting online about specific companies and when to buy stocks
- hosting hundreds of official events at properties I own
- playing golf with rich pals hundreds of times at courses I own
- frequently talking about how great all my businesses are
- encouraging my party members to do the same
- pushing dozens of foreign trademarks for my business enterprise
- orchestrating social media-driven insider trading schemes
- promoting products for the businesses of my strongest supporters
- firing anyone that doesn't pledge loyalty

- accepting millions in protection money from big businesses
- allowing nepotism and cronyism to run rampant
- pardoning the insurrectionists that tried overthrow a fair election
- pardoning white-collar criminals that supported my campaign
- offering positions of power in exchange for campaign donations
- dropping federal lawsuits against my supporters

And *so* much more!

Never mind the flagrant hypocrisy of Conservatives for all this, where is the goddamn *justice*? Most of the crimes in that wall of text happened the *first* term, and not a single politician was held accountable for anything. And now everything is just so much worse in round two of the fascist uprising in America.

The main public focus of political corruption is insider trading. Conservatives love slamming Nancy Pelosi for her casual and indirect support of insider trading, and then of course ignore all the people on *their* team doing the same shit.

You've got Republicans coming out essentially arguing how much they *need* to trade stocks to make a living. These people make nearly $200k a year at a base and work less than half the year, by the way.

Meanwhile members that violate stock trading disclosure rules are slapped with an astronomical, bank-busting fine of…$200. Wut. Oh, that usually gets *waived* too? Awesome. Incredible. Fantastic.

But there's also this "revolving door" element, where officials in all branches of government slide into high-paying lobbying jobs once they their terms end.

It's a quid pro quo — sometimes obscure and sometimes clear as day — where if a politician or judge writes friendly laws or gives friendly rulings to some company or industry, then they can be in a favorable position for a lobbying career. It happens literally all the time and the most we can do is point at it and note how corrupt it looks.

It's bullshit no matter who is doing it, and no matter which side of the political spectrum you fall. All of this corruption is bullshit. And the infuriating absence of sanctions for the flood of ethics violations is yet another "us versus them" divide of our justice system.

I want unethical Democrats arrested and financially incinerated as much as I want unethical Republicans to face such justice. That's one of the salient differences between Progressives and Conservatives.

Progressives want to hold their own criminals accountable, while Conservatives apparently make them president.

⚒ HOW WE COULD FIX IT ⚒

We'd need to rapidly and thoroughly reverse all the terribly pro-corruption crap that Republicans have pushed this time around and re-arm all those agencies. That's really the only way we are going to catch these unethical bastards.

As for insider trading, there are some options.

We could always ban individual stock trading altogether — for both the lawmakers and their immediate family. We can also institute mandatory blind trusts for all legislators so that they have no direct influence over their investments. We can shrink the disclosure window from 45 days to same-day or same-week to maintain better transparency.

And one idea I've always liked is only allowing them to invest in a special index tied directly to the U.S. economy. Its success can be determined by the broader performance of the country. If the U.S. is doing well, then so are their stock accounts.

We can also close the "revolving door" and seal it firmly shut. We need a total ban on former members of Congress from ever even *registering* as lobbyists.

And we can expand all of these ethics rules to the other two branches as well! Supreme Court justices, federal judges, Cabinet members, presidents, all of them! They should all be held to the same ethical and legal standards that every other government employee has to follow.

Yes even you, Clarence!

And then we have to *enforce* these rules.

Violators should face prison time or, at the very least, suffer heavy financial losses and be forever barred from office. They have demonstrated they do *not* have the strength of will to resist the temptations of corruption, or the purity of heart to do what is best for the people of this country! That's it! They're done!

They have been weighed in the balance and found wanting.

These politicians carelessly forgot that they are civil servants. They *WORK FOR US*! They take money from *our* paychecks to fund their salaries and benefits and travel and security and everything else!

We need *justice* for ethics breaches, not just slaps on the wrist, scathing letters, and waiting for the news cycle to roll around!

If Progressives and Conservatives can't agree on anything else, they need to agree on this.

THE SUPREME COURT

They are technically the highest authority in the U.S. justice system, so it fits with the rest of this discussion even if they don't really handle criminal law with trials and juries and all that. No, instead they handle criminal law by giving a convicted felon the keys to the country and a justice-free pass towards dictatorship.

Honestly this section shouldn't even *be* here. This court is supposed to be a relatively unbiased group of people whose only goal is a fair, objective, and *consistent* interpretation of Constitutional law. It is supposed to establish precedent and stick to the word of law regardless of which group of people hold the executive and legislative branch, and regardless of which administration got them nominated.

Nope. Instead, we have one of the most palpably partisan, contaminated, and unethical Supreme Courts in the country's history. That's what happens when you let scheming politicians fill the bench.

Conservatives have employed every trick imaginable to ram as many judges through the lower courts as possible, and why would they do anything different when it comes to the highest court?

These are *lifetime* appointments. Conservative lawmakers can ensure their stupid, evil policies are given a Supreme rubber stamp of approval for untold years to come.

And how did we get here? So much has happened it's hard to know which specific stupid, evil things led to our situation.

What I remember is Antonin Scalia dying in 2016, and Obama rightfully moving to fill his seat with the nomination of Merrick Garland (which may have been bad for Progressives anyway, but that's not the point).

Well Republicans led by Mitch McConnell, aka this era's Franz von Papen, said "Oh no no no no no you can't do *that!* The election is a measly eight months away! You need to let the American people decide our next Supreme Court Justice when the presidential election comes around!"

They obstructed the fuck out of Obama's appointment and violated long-standing precedent for how these seats are filled.

So then Trump comes along after winning his first term and fills the seat with a loyalist, Gorsuch.

Then in 2018, Anthony Kennedy retires and in comes Kavanaugh. Little crybaby, boozy frat boy, calendar-clutching Kavanaugh.

The man was credibly accused of sexual assault by multiple women, had a noted history of drinking, and there were reports of gambling and other financial debts. But the Midterms were approaching, so instead of taking the time to find a less controversial candidate, the Republicans led an *extremely* rushed and narrow investigation into the allegations and kept it all under tight White House scrutiny.

They didn't let the FBI do their fucking job. They didn't contact other sources, or corroborate stories, or interview the dozens of witnesses, or really anything that would have cleared the air.

Instead they let Kavanaugh go up there and whine that it was a Clinton revenge scheme as he pointed to some shitty old calendar to serve as proof of his innocence of rape. The investigation was raw political theater and was just pathetic to watch in real time.

This was the best Republicans could come up with to satisfy a lifetime appointment in what is supposed to be an impartial beacon of Constitutional law — a conspicuously biased man with a reported history of sexual misconduct, alcoholism, and gambling debts (which mysteriously disappeared when he took the seat).

And then we get to the favorite virtue of Republicans — hypocrisy.

In 2020, Ruth Bader Ginsburg died six freaking weeks before the presidential election. Remember how Republicans behaved when there were *eight months* left in the term? Well *they* certainly didn't remember!

Amy Coney Barrett was *barreled* through the usually-long process to get her ass in that seat as fast as legally possible.

She was ultimately confirmed eight *days* before *TRUMP LOST* the election. I yelled that so the 45-47'ers could hear.

Amy also has controversial ties with what I would describe as religious extremism. It's the kind of connection that *should* make anyone question whether she could be truly unprejudiced on matters related to the separation of church and state.

And would you look at that. The Conservatives, through some of the shadiest, most duplicitous political bullshit in our time, got a 6-3 majority in the highest court of the land.

And now we have abortion rights overturned and states clamoring to enact pregnancy tracking and Gileadic punishments for women making personal healthcare choices.

We have barefaced partisan gerrymandering being protected to maintain our counterfeit democracy.

We have the court taking on fake cases to pass rulings that more broadly allow discriminatory practices.

We have education institutions barred from using race-conscious admissions to address centuries of systemic inequality.

We have emboldened Conservative efforts to weaken unions and organized labor.

We have the erosion of the legal authority of regulatory agencies.

We have once-legal immigrants being told they are no longer welcome and court-granted blessings to racially profile civilians.

We have deeply puritanical, Christian-friendly rulings on topics like pornography, LGBTQ+ rights, and sex education.

And we have given the most criminal president in history the gift of total immunity for acts committed while in office.

They make these decisions without any deference to decades of precedent, without a shred of legal consistency, and without a care for the patently partisan optics.

They rely so heavily on the "shadow docket" and the ability to quickly push through rulings without any sort of formal, transparent, traditional discussion. Conservatives know their policies are unpopular, so they need to work in the shadows to avoid public scrutiny before they announce the next legal travesty directing our descent into fascism.

Conservatives have made this court into a farce.

They so visibly have specific, biased legislative goals in mind, and they perform world champion mental and legal gymnastics to get those viewpoints engraved into law.

They abandon precedent when it's politically convenient and they can't even stay consistent with their own internal legal logic. They declare these immensely impactful decisions for a country that didn't actually vote for them, and there's no accountability for their ethics violations.

It's a sickening parody of justice.

✖ HOW WE COULD FIX IT ✖

It's going to be really hard to fix this is a way that doesn't open the door for political retribution the next time Republicans regrettably gain control of the government. If saying "next time" is even relevant anymore to you future readers.

The big one that always gets discussed is expanding the courts. I agree that nine justices for decisions such as these feels like too few.

I'd like it expanded to something like 15 or some higher odd number.

I don't really know if stacking more people in the court would actually fix the absurd partisan separation we have, but in theory the more people you have in a group, the more diverse the opinions would get. Then again, Congress voting straight down party lines all the time sort of stomps on that theory.

Furthermore, I've always been an advocate of term limits for everything.

These Justices were given lifetime appointments by the framers of the Constitution to be insulated from political pressure. They wanted the Justices to be able to make rulings, even unpopular ones, free from legislative retribution.

The Framers also figured that lifetime appointments would mean legally consistent verdicts.

It was *supposed* to be a shield for the stability of the Constitution, regardless of whatever political squabbling is occurring within the other two branches.

Lol. Lmao even.

Yeah well that hasn't really worked out. I don't know the number of years we should limit here, but we need age and term limits.

RGB famously could have given up her seat and let Obama fill it with a better choice (even though it's likely we'd regret Garland).

It's the same dinosaur problem as in Congress. These old-ass people are clinging to life, yet decide the fate of the whole damn country. And it's even worse here since we citizens can't technically vote for them.

Maybe we could do something like an 18-year maximum term and a mandatory retirement at 70? I don't know.

We can similarly limit how many appointments a president is allowed to make in their term to put an end to the political theater nonsense.

Trump got *three* appointments in a single term. Carter, a president with actually good character, got zero.

If you have regular, scheduled appointments every two years, then each president would get two appointments per term.

You could put the Justices on a conveyor belt that rotates them out each term. They can serve 18 (or whatever max) years, or nine total terms, before they hop off the belt for good. Or whatever numbers work.

We need to also stop this shadow docket nonsense. It's only supposed to be used for emergencies, and yet this Court in particular uses it for seemingly every unpopular decree they spit out. It's preposterous and pathetic. Landmark decisions need to be fully transparent with ample time for discussion and public comment.

And we *must* implement ironclad ethics laws and a reliable way to investigate and impeach officials for violations.

There's practically nothing right now for these people, it's maddening. And some of these Justices have a super sketch side hustle going. We need this throughout all of our government of course, but the Supreme Court Justices have been skirting by on "trust me bro" for too long.

Finally, we could impose something that requires a supermajority to overturn established precedent.

Way, way too many hugely groundbreaking decisions were 5-4 majorities, and now that margin is even worse for Progressives at 6-3. Never mind how frustrating it is that the Supreme Court has been reduced to "voting down party lines" like our politicians.

Overturning precedent should be a monumental occurrence worthy of a real supermajority. Something like 7-2, or really a number like 12-3, should be required to pass rulings so game-changing.

There's so much we could do to make this court respectable again but, as with every other freaking reform in this book, we'd need way more Progressives in charge.

THE WAR ON DRUGS

This mess has been going on since like the 50s and we somehow still haven't figured out what many other developed nations have known for much longer — that drug abuse is a health problem deeply rooted in systemic socioeconomic inequality, and not a crime problem.

We could have solved this with empathy and economics. Instead, the "tough on crime" rhetoric of the Nixon and Reagan era has led to the racially targeted, widespread incarceration of primarily minorities for even the smallest drug offenses. It created a lopsided and illogical judiciary that demands disproportionate punishments for the crimes of the disadvantaged poor.

Nixon created the DEA and called drug abuse a crime issue instead of a health issue. Then Reagan came in and supported policies like mandatory minimums and civil asset forfeiture.

Reagan ushered in a war that methodically targeted minorities and created an imbalanced justice system for the crime of being non-white or poor. They literally punished the possession of crack cocaine, which is more common among poorer minorities, *100 times* more severely than the possession of the powder cocaine rich whites used. They had to know what they were doing.

The war on drugs is steeped in racism.

Republicans may be the heralds of the "tough on crime" era, but Democrats haven't helped. They were portrayed as being too *soft* on crime and sympathetic to lower class criminals. So, as usual, they decided to try swaying moderate voters — instead of aligning with Progressives — and made things even worse through the various tough-on-crime policies of their own.

The *facts* about persecution patterns didn't matter, only the picture that the Conservative propaganda painted.

And now we have this marvelously impartial system that can give minor marijuana offenders decades of prison time while some financial fraudster that harmed the livelihood of thousands can get a small fine and a few months of probation as punishment — if punished at all. We even let some of these fraudsters join Congress!

The U.S. has 5% of the world's population and like 25% of the world's prisoners because of the war on drugs, mandatory minimums, and a thorough misunderstanding and misrepresentation of the realities of drug abuse. It's simply not just.

⚒ HOW WE COULD FIX IT ⚒

Well, the good news is that even Conservatives remembered that Prohibition didn't work either, and there have been some bipartisan policy pushes aimed at finally rectifying some of the negative impacts of this foolish war on drugs, such as the Fair Sentencing Act in 2010 and the First Step Act in 2018. There have also been efforts to grant clemency to thousands of people imprisoned for minor offenses.

The bad news is that the war on drugs such as marijuana is still alive in half the country. It's tremendously inconsistent.

Some states ban certain quantities of drugs, some allow medicinal marijuana but not recreational, and some states are going straight backwards (like my terrific state) and are trying to outright ban the sale and possession of anything containing any amount of THC.

I'm sure Texas police will get right on arresting the state's more famous weed-smoking podcasters and such, right?

There are also still thousands of non-violent people in prison that were incarcerated before the latest sentencing reforms.

We need to federally decriminalize marijuana and many other forms of drug use. We need to classify drug abuse as a health and poverty issue — not a crime issue. I'd have put it in the Healthcare section if it wasn't so strongly tied to lopsided justice.

We need to reevaluate or eliminate mandatory minimums in general, with special attention to non-violent drug offenses. Many prosecutors still call for the maximum penalties for these crimes because they want to look "tough" and keep their numbers high.

We can grant judges more authority to use discretion and let them examine the circumstances of the defendants — like trauma, addiction, or poverty — before passing judgment. This would mean we need far more Progressive judges on the bench, since empathy is in short supply these days.

And most importantly, we need to work on reframing the public image of drug abuse. Other countries have shown that rehabilitation and actual treatment are far more effective and even cheaper methods of dealing with drug abuse than mass incarceration.

But our country's leaders decided to label them as criminal scum instead of people that need a support system.

Side rant here: Why do we allow alcohol consumption at 21 (or even celebrate our first drink as a rite of passage) yet vilify marijuana as the Devil's leaf?

Every pothead I've known is pretty mellow and every alcoholic I've known is a raging asshole and a danger to those around them. Anecdotal evidence, I know, but acting like getting drunk is somehow safer than getting high is some braindead logic.

Not that I expect anything else.

PRIVATE PRISONS

Can't talk about the war on drugs without bringing up private prisons. The phrase alone has such a disturbing and vile connotation to me — and probably anyone else with a conscience.

Historically, businesses have been known for mistreating workers, stifling wages, skirting regulations, and lobbying Congress all in the name of generating consistent, growing profits. It's capitalism, baby! The line needs to go up!

Despite that, our leaders, in their shockingly limitless stupidity and evil, decided that the solution to all this prison overcrowding caused by their new war on drugs was to allow private *businesses* to help handle it.

They couldn't reevaluate the policy to determine if mass incarceration was necessary. They couldn't maximize funds available to public health agencies or therapy services. They couldn't just build enough of their own, regulated infrastructure.

Instead they turned to the wealthy whites to imprison and enslave the poor of color. Where have we seen this before in U.S. history, I wonder?

The private prison industry boomed as a direct result of the war on drugs and the sudden need for mass incarcerations.

Between the anti-immigration policies from the raging right-wingers and the "tough on crime unless it's white-collar crime" hypocrites in Washington, prisons needed lots of room.

The total number of incarcerated individuals ballooned by a factor of freaking 12 in the next 40 years, and private prisons held as many as about 8% of those inmates. More than the population of a small city.

And whaddaya know — private prisons are now notorious for neglect and abuse of inmates, hiring too few and insufficiently training staff, delaying or denying healthcare for inmates, inadequate rehab and post-release planning services, fraudulent reporting, overcrowding conditions, and a hazardous lack of hygiene infrastructure among other barbaric qualities.

And to make it as exploitative as possible, these companies readily take advantage of nearly-free prisoner labor, using intimidation and retribution against those who refuse to work.

And since they are private corporations, they aren't subject to Freedom of Information Act requests and have sorely limited oversight!

They then lobby Congress to ensure the laws on the books send as many prisoners into their facilities as possible, to maintain their government contracts, and to keep their profit margins high.

And now that Conservatives have ballooned ICE's budget to be larger than the militaries of some countries, private prisons are frothing at the mouth in anticipation of the income surge.

It's truly repulsive.

Many of these people are frightened immigrants and non-violent drug offenders. They don't deserve such appalling treatment.

Even those convicted of more serious crimes still deserve some basic human dignity, don't they?

216

✖ HOW WE COULD FIX IT ✖

We should end all private prison contracts and dissolve the industry.

We also need to look at our public prisons that suffer similar shortcomings to private ones, though reforming our justice system will hopefully lower prison populations and open up more resources for that.

Furthermore, we can ban the use of prison labor if we aren't going to pay them decent wages. Prisoners shouldn't be forced to build the oligarchs' golden mountains.

Neither a country nor a business should be *incentivized* to keep the prison population high for goddamn profits. It should seek to rehabilitate and guide prisoners towards becoming valuable, well-adjusted members of society, not intentionally perpetuate a cycle of recidivism.

THE POLICE

In this country, many people do not feel safer when the police are around. Someone could be doing absolutely nothing wrong. Minding their own damn business. Following the law. And the presence of a police officer would still illicit something akin to fear or intimidation.

It's the same emotions one might feel if a known gang member entered the scene — a slight tension in the air that puts people on guard instead of leaving them at ease. And our police seem to like it that way.

You know, it's not necessarily that way in many other countries.

Police in other places are seen as respectful, knowledgeable civil servants. They are given several years of training and even degrees.

They study law, conflict resolution, human rights, psychology, communication, moral philosophy, and self-defense.

They aren't perceived as thin-tempered, lethal bullies that will ineptly escalate a bad situation and threaten your life for the smallest infractions. They don't even carry guns most of the time. The police are there to actually protect and serve, and the citizens generally know that and trust them. Generally.

Meanwhile our country's "tough on crime unless it's white-collar crime" era had both parties increasing police funding to impose mass incarcerations for their war on drugs.

The police would patrol poor, minority neighborhoods and ignore the wealthier, whiter spots (as if minorities needed any more reasons to doubt the police).

The police were militarized with new equipment and aggressive tactics.

They were given political protection through increased union muscle and friendly Washington policies.

And they were fed a rushed training regimen that painted every citizen as a potential enemy and a personal threat to be neutralized by any means necessary.

Unfortunately, none of that deserves to be in past tense because it's all still happening today, and it's gotten even worse with the bigoted Conservative rhetoric around immigration and DEI.

You can't even highlight the disparity in how police treat Black Americans by saying "Black Lives Matter" without sending an armada of Conservatives into a racist little tizzy.

We've had plentiful national incidents where police brutality, ineptitude, and misconduct were on full display.

People celebrate online when a cop gets fact-checked about the law.

People reflexively use their phones to record police actions because bodycam footage has a mysterious habit of getting damaged or lost.

People march in the streets to protest the latest tragedy of police carelessness, and the stories of police bravery and service get buried by the avalanche of scandals and failures.

Legal shields like Qualified Immunity protect officers from being sued for their misconduct.

Civil Asset Forfeiture is state-sanctioned theft allowing them to seize property without due process.

Police can investigate themselves for wrongdoing, which means the vast majority of police failures face little to no repercussions.

An officer can be fired from one precinct for gross misconduct, disappear from the limelight, and reappear at a new precinct once the dust settles.

The system defends its own, and the reputation of the police as public servants and community protectors has eroded due to insufficient training, the failures of accountability, the culture of aggression, and the reckless politics that created this problem.

Yet even as calls for reform grow louder, some "patriots" wave their Thin Blue Line flags to show support for maintaining the status quo and to protest the Progressives demanding better from our law enforcement.

Guess we just keep selling officers their misunderstood Punisher merch.

⚒ HOW WE COULD FIX IT ⚒

I want to *heavily* increase police funding. Wait, what?

In some states, you can become a police officer in 12 fucking weeks. *Three months!* Other states go up to as high as 24 weeks, but that's still *years* less education and training than many other countries require. It's unbelievable that someone can wield that much power and authority with less than half a year of training.

So we fix that. Every single police officer in the country needs to be held to a higher standard, and the foundation for that is stronger education and improved screening. If they aren't disciplined or skilled enough to get through these courses, then they don't deserve the badge and certainly not the gun.

They will be taught a similar curriculum to those other nations, with particular emphasis on U.S.-centric struggles like mental health, de-escalation, crisis intervention, community-building, gun safety, cultural competency, and ethics.

Once they become police officers, they will be periodically tested and receive continuing education on developments in psychology, communication, and other critical tools to being effective peacemakers.

They will also take regular fitness tests, mental acuity tests, and psychological evaluations to ensure they remain suitable for the responsibilities and pressures of the job.

And then there's police misconduct —

We can end Qualified Immunity and allow the police to be sued for wrongdoing. Taxpayers should no longer foot the bill for police offenses. They can buy malpractice insurance or something like doctors get, but it has to be paid for by the officers or their unions, not the citizens.

We can tighten mandates for body camera footage, evidence handling, documentation, and data transparency.

We can create independent, civilian-run review boards and third-party groups that investigate misconduct allegations.

We can then create a national registry that tracks officers that were fired or disciplined, to prevent them from taking jobs in other precincts.

And finally, and I mean this, we pay them a lot more. In some places, experienced officers are already compensated quite a bit more than the average job, between salary and other benefits. However, this isn't very consistent across the nation.

This *is* a stressful, demanding, and sometimes dangerous job! It deserves to be compensated well. With the vastly improved education, stricter acceptance and training criteria, and stronger oversight and accountability, I genuinely think they deserve to be paid very well.

This is undoubtedly a long-term, slow-ass, dauntingly expensive plan for fixing things. And yet, as someone funnier than me once said, "There's no song called 'Fuck the Fire Department'."

We'll need drastic, progressive reform to change the lyrics.

PARDON POWERS

It's just gotten out of hand, right? The legal aim behind giving the President this unilateral authority to grant pardons was *intended* to be used as a merciful check against imbalanced judgments. Now it's been violently warped into absolving political allies, staunch supporters, and campaign donors, and to systematically undermine justice.

I don't mean to say that pardon powers have never been used in shitty ways before now. It's just so much worse now.

Lincoln and Johnson pardoning Confederate leaders was a pretty bad call. Bill Clinton pardoning some treasonous tax evader was definitely corrupt. Ford pardoning Nixon for Watergate was a flagrant miscarriage of justice.

And here we are in the Trump era, where Biden feels the need to preemptively pardon his own credibly innocent son before his political opponent takes office, for fear of a baseless witch hunt.

Trump, to the surprise of no one paying attention, has exhibited the pinnacle illustration of the abuse of pardon power and has reignited the debate about its existence and the need for reform.

Some of the most noteworthy and corrupt Trump pardons include:

- A sheriff that was accused of anti-immigrant practices and violated a court order to stop racially profiling Latinos.

- A Conservative commentator and loyalist that violated campaign finance and election law.

- Another Trump-supporting sheriff that accepted tens of thousands in bribes to deputize several businessmen.

- A nursing home executive that evaded paying millions of dollars in taxes — whose scummy mother donated a fortune to Trump and other Republicans.

- His son-in-law's father, who was convicted of tax evasion, breaking campaign finance law, and witness tampering.

- His former national security advisor that plead guilty to lying twice to the FBI about his communications with Russia during an election interference investigation.

- His former campaign chairman that was convicted of bank fraud, tax fraud, and conspiracy charges related to the Russia election interference investigation.

- A close advisor and longtime Republican operative, who was convicted of obstructing a congressional investigation into…you guessed it…the Russia election interference case.

- His former chief strategist, who was charged with defrauding the donors looking to pay for his unfinished border wall.

- A famous couple that was found guilty of cheating banks out of tens of millions and committed numerous tax crimes — whose daughter spoke at the RNC and campaigned fervently for Trump.

- Sweeping clemency to nearly 1600 Trump supporters charged in the January 6 insurrection at our Capitol, including hundreds of people that assaulted the police and invaded the personal offices of our elected representatives.

I mean look at that fucking list and tell me that pardon powers don't need serious limitations. And that's only a handful!

Commit whatever crimes you want as long as you donate truckloads of money and support the right campaign!

Defy court orders, steal from the IRS, lie to the FBI, take countless bribes, assault our Capitol police, whatever! Pardons for anyone who kisses the ring!

It's a white-collar crime spree, and I'd bet the farm there'll be more by the time this raging book is published.

Conservatives, is this what you want from the "party of law and order"?

How could any reasonable voter look at a list like this and see anything but model classism and authoritarianism?

✖ HOW WE COULD FIX IT ✖

Pardons need oversight. Simple as that.

There should be an independent clemency review board empowered to examine the facts of each case with full transparency and determine whether a pardon would breach public trust.

We also need to bar presidents from pardoning political allies, outspoken supporters, major donors, or anyone else whose connection to them represents a clear conflict of interest. Let the review board handle those.

Hell, if it were up to me, I'd let the public vote on pardons. I know voter turnout is pretty atrocious (which I'd want to fix too), but if the president was going to pardon them without our input anyway, what's the harm in letting the public decide?

You could do them all together maybe once or twice a year.

Give their name, their crime, the justification for a pardon, and any other relevant information and let the public decide!

You could even bundle cases for mass clemency arrangements.

It feels like something that could give the nation more faith in the justice system if white-collar criminals and frothing insurrectionists weren't going free because the most corrupt president of all time was bribed with cash and constancy.

Either way this shit has gone overboard.

I'm just waiting for our partisan, fascist-flirting Supreme Court to decide the president can pardon themselves.

<u>CLOSING RANT</u>

This country has such a cruel, cringeworthy approach to handling and perceiving criminals, especially non-violent ones.

If you're a rich white person, then your situation is complex and forgivable and whatever harm you did doesn't need to be measured by the gravity of your crimes or the count of lives you hurt.

If you're a poor minority, then the problem is *you* and the systemic failures around you have nothing to do with your personal responsibility to follow the law.

The rich get lectures and pardons and the opportunity to rehabilitate. The poor get prison, forced labor, and a lifetime of regret.

We'll drug test people on welfare, but not the shapers of our society.

We need to drastically restructure how justice functions in this country, from the badged enforcers all the way to the highest courts.

When the whole system becomes a partisan mockery, it shouldn't be surprising if the commonfolk stop caring about the law altogether.

I'd bet that if every topic I rant about in this depressing book were actually solved that the criminal population among the poor would drastically decline.

Systemic poverty, systemic bigotry, physical health, mental health, education, affordable housing, gun control, justice reform…these are the sorts of issues to be fixed if we want a nation that actually cares about reducing crime instead of one that only pretends to care.

RELIGION

RELIGION

Both of my parents were raised in the church, though neither of them stayed hardcore Bible-thumpers and we only rarely attended when I was young. We said our prayers before dinner and bed, with little else.

Despite this, I have still gathered a gradient of exposure to religion — mostly Christianity and therefore Christians. I have been to numerous services for a large variety of sects including Methodist, Church of Christ, Southern Baptist, Episcopalian, Presbyterian, Catholic, and Non-denominational or "Bible" churches. I even visited a Synagogue and a Buddhist Temple when I went to college.

With that background noted, my experiences with the church have propelled me to agnosticism. This means that I do not have enough evidence to decide what to believe is true.

Catholicism could be right, Protestantism could be right, Islam could be right, Hinduism could be right, Judaism could be right, or any other religion could be right. Maybe they all have pieces that are right. Maybe none of them do. I do not know, and that's the point.

I'm not going to sit here and pretend that I have the answer to the end of all things. That my spiritual worldview is the one infallible truth. That all other faiths and creeds, all other religious texts, and all other stories are wrong, and that my outlook is the only path to a peaceful afterlife.

I do believe that nearly every religion has at least some *historical* truth behind it and that there are fair reasons why each of them formed. But I do not believe in any of them with the strength of faith necessary to say I am religious. And frankly, I have become wholly disillusioned with the idea of organized religion over the years.

It *has* done some good — early morality systems, public service, poetry, music, architecture, culture, community, etc. And there have been miraculous moments in history where the religious masses have been shepherded by voices of compassion and peace, where grand humanitarian works and powerful movements have shaped the world we share for the better.

Yet it also can't be denied that religion and its leaders have played pivotal roles in some of the most monstrous, shameful events of our history. The holy wars, the harrowing inquisitions, the zealous genocide, the ceaseless geopolitical conflict — all rooted in the evils of sectarianism and the corrupted obligations of faith. And it's all still occurring today everywhere we look.

Religion has also been a noteworthy counterweight to the forces of scientific progress and the pull of our true potential.

Historically, many Churches supervised education and suppressed the pursuit of new worldviews and empirical exploration. They imprisoned and executed scientists and scholars for daring to question the grand theological design. They would shun and abandon innovative solutions to a growing world of complex problems.

I've wondered if humanitarian efforts and compassionate movements would have been needed at all had the world's most fervent fanatics never been granted any authority.

If religion had been dedicated purely to community and enlightenment, with its dogmatic and insular voices silenced rather than celebrated, would humanity have endured the same scale of untold suffering?

If the very concept of a divine right to rule had never taken hold, would world leaders have been chosen on merit alone?

If the untold wealth and resources of religious institutions had been distributed differently, would we be more educated and advanced today?

We can't know all that, but the point is that religion has never been an entirely benevolent force of peace and progress. Its long history is a balancing act between extremist regression and enlightened advancement perpetuated by the whims of the wealthiest and most connected religious leaders.

I don't believe it deserves credit for "all the good it's done" without also acknowledging its central role in dividing and stifling humanity.

Regardless, the sad truth is that religion is very frequently used as a tool for tyrants. It remains an immensely effective instrument for the control and manipulation of vulnerable people seeking truth and meaning in an unforgiving world.

In exchange for obedient faith and devout servitude to the "one true cause," followers are promised intangible rewards in an unknowable afterlife. This promise offers comfort and a sense of belonging that can feel impossible to achieve, even on this crowded Earth.

This gift of community and purpose is so often warped, giving some the self-righteous conviction to judge all those that believe differently. Anyone outside their ethnocentric theological paradigm is condemned to persecution and damnation.

In the worst times, this conviction has ignited a passion for forced conversions, oppression, and violence against those deemed 'unworthy' by the prevailing dogma.

It should be telling that it doesn't really matter which religion I'm ranting about — every single major faith has, at some point, been used to justify the oppression or domination of another people.

Whenever religion claims authority over a nation, it's normally the extremists who sit at the helm. Some might argue that extremist viewpoints shouldn't represent the whole, and I would usually offer a nuanced agreement.

But that argument falls flat when those fanatical figures are given the power to write our laws, lead our courts, edit our textbooks, influence our children, and spread their militant faith outside the walls of their holy barracks by the favor and patronage of a population.

Anyone who offers financial, political, or even passive support for these cruel zealots' platforms bears responsibility for the damage they cause. Just as the Germans had a word for *everyone* who supported the atrocities of their extremist right-wing party.

Conservatives who've made it this far (good job, by the way!) — are you raging right now? Are you asking how someone that is *clearly* a radical leftist can *possibly* say that extremists are harmful? Such a hypocrite, right?

Yeah y'all, wanting to help the most vulnerable populations, imbue empathy into our children, guard the natural environment, and level the hopelessly tilted scales of socioeconomic equality is real *extremist* shit.

Anyway, maybe I'm wrong about it all.

Maybe without religion we'd have a bunch of savage, distrusting, hateful nationalist bigots who only answer to the grand authority of the almighty dollar.

Our leaders would be the wealthiest people in our land, and their dynasty would linger by the holy grace of compound interest.

We'd trample and denigrate the poor for failing to win a rigged game and claw their way out of generational poverty.

We'd instigate foreign wars of both trade and territory to claim resources and maintain our global dominance.

And we'd undermine countless progressive initiatives or policies for simply being too expensive or time-consuming.

Sound familiar, Conservatives?

CONSERVATIVE CHRISTIANS

I posit that not a single modern Conservative can genuinely claim to follow the core teachings of Christianity. The two ideologies are fundamentally and categorically incompatible no matter what denominational lens you look through.

This preachy book has taken a pretty exhaustive dive into what Conservatism really is in this country — the policies it champions, the fights it chooses, the people it serves, and the leaders it elects.

So, let's examine what Christianity is all about and determine if Conservatives have even touched their faith's required reading.

What better place to begin than the Ten Commandments? These are the building blocks of Christian "law" — the Old Testament ethical, moral, and religious standard that all Christians should broadly follow if they want to get into Heaven. In the New Testament, Jesus' word provides critical additional context to these laws so that his followers have a deeper, clearer understanding of what it means to follow Christ and how to practice what is preached.

Here we go, with some paraphrasing.

I.   You shall have no other gods before Me.

This first one is simple to do, right? You can only worship the one true God. Reject idolatry, reject polytheism, and place your ultimate loyalty in God alone.

The Conservative obsession with patriotism and the nationalistic fervor they hold for their infallible version of America is not exclusive worship to God. Their unquestioning allegiance to a political ideology is not exclusive worship to God. Their sycophantic, spineless devotion to certain political leaders is not exclusive worship to God.

Hmm…Numero uno here and Conservatives aren't doing well.

II.   You shall make no idols.

Okay this is a little more nuanced. This is saying not to make any physical representations of God or other gods to worship, right?

What are the physical idols of Conservatism then?

Could it be a little AR-15 pin? A Thin Blue Line flag? A Bible sold as merch by your favorite politician? A golden Trump effigy embossed with "In Trump We Trust"? How about a bright red hat?

Seems like there are plenty of little objects floating around representing more than just patriotism or ideology or fandom.

They look an awful lot like idols of worship to me.

III.   You shall not take the name of the Lord in vain.

This doesn't just mean you can't say "God damn it". It means that when you evoke the name of God, it had better be in sincere reverence to the teachings of Jesus.

It means not to swear, but also not to lie or be hypocritical when speaking of God.

Conservatives love to throw out accusations of "virtue signaling" when they are by far the worst offenders of performative morality, and in a way that borders on the sacrilegious.

Wearing a huge, bejeweled cross as you lie through your teeth for the god of your political party is taking the Lord's name in vain.

Pressing your followers to vote Republican during a sermon is taking the Lord's name in vain.

Tear-gassing innocent crowds to pose for photos while holding a Bible upside down is taking the Lord's name in vain.

Putting the cute little Christian fish next to your wrap of Joe Biden hogtied in the truck bed is taking the Lord's name in vain.

I could honestly make another one my verbose lists on the ways Conservative "Christians" take the Lord's name in vain, but I've made my point.

IV.   Keep the Sabbath day holy.

Okay so Sunday is off limits. Or is it Saturday? Is it God's particular rest day or just any day of the week? They're kinda inconsistent with this one. Let's pretend that the nearly ubiquitous practice of holding Christian worship services on Sunday means that Sunday is the holy day of the Sabbath. It is a day to rest and reflect on worship and the immutable word of God.

So do Conservatives call to end all commercial ventures on Sunday? Do they strive for the workers' right to embrace the day as commanded?

Of course not. There's post-church dining and Sunday football to get to!

I'll admit this one is a stretch, but the premise is there.

When you actively push for economic systems that prevent workers from having the time or energy for proper rest and worship — on Sunday or any other day — then that's not respecting the Sabbath.

V.   Honor your father and your mother.

Respect the elderly, and more broadly respect family.

I see Conservatives honor this commandment by cutting healthcare and financial aid for seniors, separating children from their loved ones at the border, and severing childcare benefits for new parents.

Classic respect.

VI.   You shall not murder.

Don't kill people. And logically this also means one shouldn't support systems that kill people, right? It's a call to value all life, not only in the literal sense, but also in how society cares for the vulnerable.

And in Matthew 5:21-22, Jesus expanded on this to include even being angry or contemptuous towards others.

Yet Conservative policy routinely shirks this principle.

Conservatives are the party of passionate militarism and cutting aid to victims of violence and tragedy. Lots of death there.

Conservatives are the party that fiercely clings to their gun rights despite ongoing mass shootings and assassinations. People with guns can — and this is true — more easily kill other people.

Conservatives uphold a healthcare system so disgraceful that millions of people suffer and die needlessly. Death by neglect and denied medical care is still death.

Conservatives are the strongest advocates of oppressive policing and capital punishment. More anger and death.

Conservatives support a rhetoric that routinely dehumanizes both its political opponents and virtually every single vulnerable population. Rings rather contemptuous, that.

I don't know — for a movement that routinely claims a moral and spiritual high ground, Conservative politics today condones an alarming amount of violence, hate, death, and outright disregard for life.

Must be that Christian love they talk so much about.

VII.   You shall not commit adultery.

Unlike Conservatives, I'm not really looking to get all up in your bedroom business. But tell me why they have, three times now, nominated a leader with a widely known history of infidelity?

Remember, the national debate wasn't about whether or not Donald Trump paid hush money to conceal an affair with an adult film star while his third wife nursed his fourth child. The debate was over whether he violated campaign finance laws in doing so. These are the family values I'm talking about!

Ah, I see the pundits would rather just keep the focus on condemning the LGBTQ+ community and that sort of "sexual deviance". Got it.

VIII.   You shall not steal.

Boy this could be interpreted in a bunch of ways, huh?

The idea of theft is easily broadened beyond just petty theft.

It includes stealing money through fraud, exploitation, or malicious business practices.

It includes scooping up family homes or plundering natural resources.

It includes robbing children and adults of a quality education.

It includes depriving disadvantaged groups of aid and protection.

It includes snatching life itself through unjust laws and biased systems.

If anyone can read this heathenish book and come away thinking that Conservative politics isn't positively *rife* with theft of all kinds, then maybe they skipped a few chapters.

Conservative policies steal from the poor and give to the rich. They steal representation. They steal fair wages and job benefits. They steal healthcare. They steal school funding. They steal natural resources. They steal years from the innocent immigrants and the queer communities and the non-violent drug offenders.

These are *all* thefts of a kind.

IX.   You shall not bear false witness.

Don't lie. Tell the truth and only the truth. Very easy.

Do we really have to examine all the ways Conservative voices and media figures spread lies? Entire elements of their platform have leaned heavily on deception and propaganda since the beginning.

The number going around for the count of times that Trump gave misleading or outright false statements in his first term alone was over 30,500 — a number widely reported and fact-checked. His record is climbing even faster in his second term!

Fox News has repeatedly been caught doctoring photos for stories they air, and for using outdated or irrelevant video clips to obscure the truth of various events.

They've been through high-profile lawsuits for false reporting, including a landmark settlement for knowingly spreading misinformation about voting machines and election fraud.

And that's just Fox, which some Conservatives think isn't right-wing *enough* for their tastes.

Right-wing networks consistently push distorted or incomplete narratives to shape public opinion.

They bear a *lot* of false witness. That is, they are lying goddamn liars.

X. You shall not covet.

This is a challenge against envy and greed. It's not just about lusting after your neighbor's wife.

It's about being happy with what you have and sharing excess with your fellows and the needy.

It's about contentment and generosity.

It's about resisting the pull of abundance.

Instead, Conservative policy celebrates consumerism to the point of glorifying and electing billionaires.

Its media preaches a vile resentment of the "other" and fuels outrage that the so-called "unworthy" are offered dignities like healthcare, housing, fair wages, or basic human rights.

There is a constant agitation over taxes being used to help "the wrong people" and applause when military force is used against neighbors of different backgrounds.

Conservative voters support their leaders' plans to cut programs that offer aid to refugees of war, disaster, or persecution because they see it as robbing from their own coffers.

It's reflective of a common "zero-sum" perspective among most Conservatives, where giving to others means taking from themselves.

These are *deeply* covetous viewpoints.

Alright so Conservatives are pretty much 0 for 10 on Biblical law.

"That's not right, though, you can't do that! Jesus came and fulfilled the ceremonial law! It's the New Covenant now!"

Except Jesus didn't fly in and nullify the Ten Commandments. He elaborated on their meaning and gave clarity to the heart of the words. Jesus *embodied* the Commandments, and, through His example, good Christians could see what the law of God represents.

But fine! I interpret Matthew 5:17-20 differently, but fine. We can focus only on the teachings of the New Testament. I'm *sure* they'll make Conservative policy look better!

The Book of Matthew in particular gives a very clear picture on the ethical teachings of Jesus, and what one could consider to be the new set of commandments for Christians to follow.

We've got Matthew 22:37-38, which says to love God in your heart, soul, and mind. Very much like the first Commandment, which we discussed before.

Then that verse continues with Matthew 22:39-40 and says to love your neighbor as yourself.

This includes outsiders like immigrants.

This includes enemies, like political adversaries and foreign powers.

This includes the vulnerable, like minorities and all the other marginalized groups I've mentioned.

We see this again in Luke 10:25-37 and the parable of the Good Samaritan. Jesus tells a story to highlight the importance of mercy and helping those in need, as well as the dishonor for those who ignore the call for aid.

These are described as the key commandments of Jesus. Love God, and love your neighbor. So where exactly do Conservative policies reflect this essential Christian virtue?

Matthew 7:12 lays out the Golden Rule: Do unto others as you would have them do unto you. It's one of the fundamentals of empathy.

Are Conservatives known for their empathy? Are they known for treating all people with compassion and fairness? Or are they known for seeing empathy as a New Age woke form of weakness?

Matthew 6:1-8 cautions against the self-righteous hypocrisy of publicly announcing your faith with "trumpets" and striving to be seen worship.

And yet how often do we see prominent Conservative figures loudly proclaiming their faith while supporting policies that cause others harm?

They'll take to social media platforms and all-caps shout their love for Jesus first and Trump second.

They'll let their Christian symbols dangle off their necks as quiet signals of perceived moral superiority.

They'll occupy street corners and hold signs vilifying women and minorities, warning of eternal damnation.

They trumpet *constantly*.

Matthew 6:14-15 states the value of forgiving both those that sin against us and those that sin against others.

It very plainly says that failing to forgive others will block you from forgiveness yourself.

Conservative policies reflect judgment, not grace! Forgiveness is replaced with condemnation and a drive to punish and exclude perceived enemies of the faith. This strongly conflicts with the whole "Love your enemies" thing in Matthew 5:44. Then Matthew 7:1 also firmly warns against similar judgmental attitudes.

You want me to stop cherry-picking Matthew? Alright fine, let's look at the good ol' Gospel of the Poor, i.e. Luke:

Luke 6:20-26 says that the poor and the hungry are blessed but give woe to the rich and the "well-fed".

Luke 12:13-21 tells the story of a man that hoards both wealth and harvest, and God calls the man a fool for being so gluttonous.

Luke 16 highlights how you cannot serve both God and money. It recounts the tale of a rich man that ignored the needs of a poor beggar — and when the rich man died, he was tormented in the afterlife while the beggar sat with God in Heaven.

Luke 3:11 demands for people to give up their excess clothing and food to the destitute.

Luke 19:1-10 has a sleazy, wealthy tax collector giving up half his misbegotten gains and repaying anyone he cheated "four times" over. And Jesus approves with a thumbs up and a "this guy gets it" vibe.

Luke 18:25 suggests that a freaking camel would have an easier time getting through the eye of a sewing needle than a rich person would have getting into Heaven. It really doesn't get much clearer than that how Jesus feels about the wealthy and their treatment of the poor.

Tell me, Conservatives, what policies do you support that make you champions of the underprivileged?

Do you speak woe to the billionaires?

Do you strive to ensure the poor and needy are cared for?

Do you welcome your disadvantaged neighbors with open, loving arms?

Oh…you do the exact opposite of all that at every voting opportunity. That camel will need to defy some physics for you.

Jesus undoubtedly calls on His followers to prove their love of God by showing equal love and compassion for enemies, for the poor, for the hungry, and for the helpless.

He repetitively preaches a commandment of empathy and social justice.

He vehemently condemns the corrupt, the materialistic, the exploitative, the violent, and the hypocritical.

It's direct opposition to the religious and economic systems that misuse God's name for their own gain.

And yet look at Conservative practices and policies. They represent everything that had Jesus flipping tables.

What I'm really saying here is that Jesus was a liberal-ass Progressive.

Here's a handful more verses from both Testaments!

1 John 3:17 | Exodus 22:21 | Leviticus 19:33-34 | Leviticus 24:22 | Jeremiah 22:3-5 | Deuteronomy 27:19 | Mark 10:11 | Mark 10:21 | Luke 6:27-28 | Acts 2:44-45 | Acts 4:34-37 | Numbers 5:18-28 | 1 Timothy 6:5-11 | Proverbs 14:31 | Proverbs 12:22 | John 8:7 | Genesis 2:15

So if Conservatives don't follow reasonable interpretations of the Old Testament Ten Commandments, and they don't follow the unmistakable lessons of Jesus Christ in the New Testament, then what is left of authentic Christian practice in that movement?

Nothing. It's really that simple! They are *not* Biblical Christians.

They may *believe* they are living out Christian values. They may go to a Christian church and sing Christian hymns and hear Christian sermons and perform Christian works in their community...

But when they step into the world and support a platform built on fear, division, lies, greed, harm, exclusion, and so much else that opposes the guidance in their rulebook, then they shouldn't be surprised if they are unwelcome in Heaven and the Pearly Gates remain sealed shut.

If a poor, brown prophet preaching empathy for the needy and criticizing the rich rose today, would Conservatives listen and change, or would they crucify him all over again?

RELIGION IN GOVERNMENT

The U.S. has been molded by the hand of religion since its birth, and recently the real extremists have gained a terrifying concentration of authority, largely thanks to relentless Conservative legislative efforts.

We call them "Christian white nationalists". Y'all-Qaeda. Vanilla ISIS. Talibangelicals. Yeehawdists. Okay I'm done. Thanks, Reddit.

Conservatives, with their goldfish-memory and apparent allergy to real history, forgot that this country was founded on religious freedom, and that Christianity is not, and never has been, the "national religion" of the United States.

The First Amendment to the Constitution says, "Congress shall make no law respecting an establishment of religion, or prohibiting the free exercise thereof." It is the separation of church and state.

Say it with me again for the red-hats in the back of the class — the *Separation. Of. Church. And. State.*

And yet here we are, still trying to set ourselves apart from those "godless Commies".

We have God on our money, we have God in our pledge, and we have God in many oaths. It doesn't say *which* God, mind you, however it is a capital 'G', which to me indicates a monotheistic God and excludes any religions that think in little 'g' gods.

Winning an elected office while identifying as anything other than a professing Christian is considered newsworthy.

Showing criticism of organized religion can sink any political campaign.

Support of Protestant, Catholic, and Jewish interests remains an unspoken requirement for holding office.

And as Conservatives creep our country closer to theocratic authoritarianism, it's gotten much worse.

We have churches openly campaigning for Republicans during sermons.

We have elected leaders and high-ranking officials with deep personal ties to extremist Christian organizations.

We have Christian special interest groups like the ADF working dangerously close to legislators to enact religion-friendly laws.

We have a Supreme Court issuing overtly religious rulings on cases involving abortion and public-school prayer.

We have a Christian-filled government floating the scheme of using taxpayer money to establish religious charter schools.

We have legislation being pushed that would allow your supervisor at work to legally proselytize to you.

We even have the current admin forming a fucking *Faith Office* to "eradicate anti-Christian bias". Lemme just check that box in the 14 points of fascism real quick.

99% of Congressional Republicans and 80% of Democrats identify as some form of Christian!

This religion has such an astounding amount of influence in every branch of our government, and yet some Conservatives still cry about "anti-Christian bias." The real anti-Christian threats in office are these very Conservatives and their throbbing persecution complexes.

The Christian religion has a stranglehold on our government and scoffs at the thought of true separation.

🛠 HOW WE COULD FIX IT 🛠

I'd want to do what the Constitution says we should do, and keep government and religion explicitly separated.

This means removing any religious language on our money, in our pledges, our oaths, and anywhere else related to the government.

It means prohibiting government workers from making religious statements while operating in an official capacity.

It means establishing anti-religion ethics laws that keep our tax-paid representatives and justices from supporting or colluding with religious groups while in office.

It means impeaching those that refuse to follow these religious-neutrality laws.

It also means an overhaul of the tax policies many churches have long exploited due to an embarrassing lack of oversight. We need to distinguish genuine religion from tax avoidance shelters and fraud.

Churches and similar religious institutions should be treated like any other nonprofit organization that benefits from public infrastructure.

They should be required to apply and qualify for tax-exempt status with detailed financial disclosure to our new well-funded IRS. Tax-exempt status should be tied to charitable work, not just their sometimes false identity as a religion.

We can also cap allowances and impose partial property taxes so that small towns with dozens of churches aren't starved of income.

They should also be subject to regular audits and any for-profit activities managed by the church should be taxed as business income, with a priority focus on shady shit like mega-churches and Scientology.

Those fuckers need to be investigated, for real.

And finally, we should be penalizing churches that offer any form of political campaign support whatsoever by revoking tax-exempt status.

Christians will frame this as an attack on their faith because they are so deeply entrenched in our government that separating the two feels like a violation. They are *supposed* to be separated!

RELIGION IN SCHOOL

School is about learning facts. It's about math, science, health, fine arts, language, history, and technology. It's about preparing students for becoming functional, intelligent members of a working society, not imposing gospels of faith.

It's about learning how to learn, not preaching how to live.

Yet Christian Conservatives have long been trying to inject their ideology into our children's curriculum.

They want the Ten Commandments displayed in school lobbies.

They propose Bible literacy classes under the guise of "heritage".

They lobby for courses to frame Bible stories as central to history.

They fight to ban any acknowledgment of LGTBQ+ people in school under the hateful, deceitful justification of "protecting the kids".

Science classes should teach the realities of evolution — not the mystical magic of creationism.

History classes should teach verifiable events of our past — not a collection of religious allegories and parables.

Health classes should teach accurate information about sex, anatomy, and identity — not shame, fear, and chastity.

These are tax-supported educational institutions, and religion has no right to spread its views to our kids there. These are the same people, mind you, screaming about the "Liberal indoctrination" they think occurs at universities. We need facts, not feelings.

It's always Christianity here too, isn't it? They'd faint if we tried to teach the cultural significance of the Quran or allowed a teacher to do midday prayers towards Mecca during class.

If history classes aren't teaching the stories of Muhammad or any other religious figures, then they sure as shit shouldn't be teaching about Jesus or other Bible characters.

✖ HOW WE COULD FIX IT ✖

Same path as the last section, but for public schools.

We need to heavily reinforce the separation of church and state as it relates to school curriculum and its officials.

We can write stronger federal laws prohibiting religious influence in schools and impose strict secular standards.

We can promote more transparency and choice regarding any religion-coded content in the curriculum. Scientific fact is not religion, morons.

We can improve accountability for school district leadership to uphold these laws and prevent ethics breaches.

And we can improve protections and resources for the whistleblowers and activists that expose violations.

We'd probably have to expand the Supreme Court to get the lot of this done since most of the current Justices have strong personal religious convictions, and calling that court an "impartial body" is a stale joke at this point.

They have very intentionally, piece by piece, eroded the old legal safeguards against religious imposition and paved the way for much of the curiously Christianity-centric legislation we see today. So they can be reformed too.

CLOSING RANT

I don't actually have a problem with personal religion, despite how this whole section reads. I know how important a sense of belonging and purpose can be for so many. I quite clearly like the idea of helping the needy and weakening the dreadful side-effects of the wealth-centered world we wander.

I admire what religions like Christianity are *supposed* to be about.

My problem is with *organized* religion and the growing influence it has on our government and laws.

RELIGION

My problem is with religious fanatics seeking to convert or condemn anyone that sees the universe differently.

My problem is with giving "God" credit for everything good that happens, and blaming "the Devil" for everything else.

My problem is with hypocrisy and cruelty posing as "God's love".

My problem is with Conservatives claiming the Christian label while backing policies antithetical to Christ's teachings.

Anyone with a shred of knowledge about the history of religious extremism and the dangers of theological uprisings should be afraid of our current political situation and the grand religious ethno-state vision some Conservatives terrifyingly desire for America.

These "Christian" nationalists have already infiltrated Congress and the Courts. They've succeeded in pushing legislation and policy to reflect their Jesus-defying worldview, and it's only a matter of time before their unchecked coup will lead to the establishment of our first national creed.

They will surely then threaten the rights and lives of anyone that believes in a different faith or defies the new world order.

But again, Conservatives are not acting as Christians anymore. They cannot support the policies they support, or feel the hate they feel, and still claim to follow Christ as He is written.

Their religion is just a tribal label, and their leaders are, at best, merely political opportunists using faith as a convenient weapon of control.

Their true creed is capitalism and country. It is a cult of America.

And I suspect the Christian God isn't blessing the U.S.A. today.

FINAL RANT

FINAL RANT

So that's all, folks. Those are the main topics I've wanted to rant about. I know I didn't cover anywhere close to everything that needs fixing. There's just so much wrong and I couldn't hit it all.

I didn't talk much about military waste because I don't have enough to say about it. We need to audit the ever-loving hell out of our "defense" budget, and it's frustrating that we have enough money to be the world's police, yet we can't take care of our own citizens. Maybe the tax reforms in here would fix the shortfalls.

I didn't talk much about the depressing state of journalism and the decades of capitulation to fascism and oligarchy — and most destructively their gutless sane-washing of stochastic terrorists like Trump and his ilk.

They share far and wide every stupid fucking word coming out of the hateful, ignorant mouths of these Conservative figureheads, and barely do anything to push back on the constant flow of lies. They cave to frivolous lawsuits that trample all over free speech. They cancel successful shows because the snowflake in charge gets his feelings hurt.

Journalism needs a remodel, but it's been consolidated so badly that like six companies own everything in that space. Busting monopolies and bringing back the Fairness Doctrine would be a start, but what else?

I didn't talk about the Israel-Gaza crisis that's a hot button topic of today. I personally believe the U.S. is complicit in the suffering of a people and it is being loosely justified by the actions of a handful of zealots. I think branding peace advocates as "anti-Semitic" is offensive to the term. And I think if religious extremism didn't exist then the land could be easily shared.

I don't have a solution to an ancient conflict, though. We could simply...ya know...stop funding genocide.

There are a bunch of different policy notes I wanted to mention, reforms I'd want implemented, etc. But either I failed to find a good place for them, I didn't have enough to say, or I found I wasn't knowledgeable enough for a good argument.

With that said, if you read all of this and are now pissed off that I didn't comment on the issue most dear to your heart, then I am truly sorry. Conservative policies just ruin so goddamn much that it can be tough to remember or discuss it all in one place. Plus the book was getting long.

Yet the Right will happily ignore the copious failings of their ideology and focus on the "whataboutisms" aimed at Progressive opinions and lifestyles, relying on fringe gotcha moments and clickbait.

These sorts of "intellectual" walking Dunning-Kruger Conservatives and the smug self-described "Centrists" will dismiss the whole platform of Progressives because we can't fight every single battle with an equal measure of force and fervor.

"You'll protest the oil industry's greed, but still drive a car!?"
"You'll fight the rise of corporate surveillance, but still use your phone?"
"You'll berate billionaires for existing, but still buy stuff!?"
"Checkmate, libtard. Like and subscribe."

Wanting to focus on renewables and slowly phase out oil dependence does not mean we should sell the cars we need to get to work.

Wanting tech bros to stop careening us into a cyberpunk AI-overlord corpo-dystopia does not mean we can't use modern technology.

Wanting the wealthy to fucking pay their fair share through taxes doesn't mean we have to avoid participating in commerce.

I mean, I'm still using self-publishing services like Amazon for this.

If that somehow invalidates the general principle of my rants to you, then you were probably never the sort to be swayed anyway. Not that this book was written to change your mind.

Again, these arguments are just disingenuous attempts to diminish the intent of Progressive policy and dismiss Progressive voices. It's an excuse Conservatives frequently use to remain blissfully opposed to positive change and blind to the half-witted horrors of their actions.

Sure, the supporters of Liberal/Leftist/Progressive ideology aren't perfect — myself very much included. Their passion is strong, but their focus can be disjointed, their words can be poorly chosen, and their methods can be tinged with aggression. Like this book, ha!

But their heart is in the right place, which is more than I can say for most of today's Conservatives. Progressives want what the name suggests — progress for the country. Conservatives move us backwards.

I'd call Progressives the true patriots if that word wasn't spiritually tainted. Right-wingers have turned being a "patriot" into a worthless label that might as well say "Conservative white nationalist". They're just fascists masquerading as country-loving citizens.

Real patriotism isn't about pride. Real patriotism is about recognizing the atrocities that got you here and holding your country to a higher standard. It's about aspiring to a better future for *everyone,* regardless of skin tone, religion, gender, sexuality, and origin story. It's about truly honoring those that paved the way for that future.

You can't just hug the flag, write a slogan, and call it a day.

Conservatives are America First, though! You know, except for anything that matters for improving everyday American lives. Tell me how that's true patriotism.

There was a time when Conservatives may have been more reasonable, but that era is long gone.

It's not like when Trump passes that a "better" Republican will replace him. There are no better Republicans anymore. There will be smarter ones. Maybe somehow more depraved ones. But none will be any better for the country or our lives.

They'll try to distance themselves from the monster they nurtured and pretend like they're a brand new party. Then they'll keep telling their lies and spreading their hate and nominating their like-minded judges until the country either suddenly implodes or it slowly withers and dies.

And the U.S. *is* sick and has been for some time. Only in the last decade have the symptoms of racism, anti-intellectualism, nationalism, religious extremism, government corruption, wealth inequality, and the overall goals and outcomes of Conservative policy finally manifested into a true fascist disease.

Progressives are out here like under-equipped T-cells trying desperately to keep the host alive. And we're losing. Some days I wish for a good ol' amputation — to sever the infected flesh and be done with it.

Meanwhile Democrats preach about how "divided and bitter" we are as if that's somehow not a painfully obvious outcome to everything that's been happening the past 10+ years.

No shit we're divided and bitter! A huge swath of this country are stupid, evil fascist enablers living in a mental illness-soaked fever dream and the Democrats played a noticeable part in coddling them and amplifying their insufferable voices!

It is *long* past the time for making political peace with these people. The possibility of legislative compromise shattered the moment Trump was allowed back on the ballot after everything he's done.

We need to stop taking the high road and start smearing Republican's noses in the messy shits they leave. They *love* to vote in lockstep with their dear leader's desires on various legislation packages, and then immediately try to renounce or separate from their own fucking votes. "Oh, whoops I didn't read the bill. Sorry, constituents!"

They *know* what they are doing. They know! And they shouldn't be allowed to keep our taxes while washing their hands of accountability.

But no, Democrats are so worried about decorum, and playing fair, and seniority, and a lot of other shit that's pointless when you're in a war against fascism. Shove those strongly-worded letters right up your ass and get to forging a real political arsenal!

Democracy *needs* to be weaponized against tyrants! Trump and his minions should have been rotting in federal prison while the Democrats released a flood of legislation to safeguard the country. Instead, they sewed white flags and handed him a second, somehow worse term.

The reality is that the Cold War never ended, and Russia's done a damn good job playing the long game. Seriously ask yourself how you could destroy a country without using military might, and then compare notes with Conservative policies and talking points:

Buy some elite fools. Tell them to write policies that make the people dumber, sicker, and poorer. Order those bought leaders to abandon their longest and strongest alliances. Grant the oligarchs as much voice and influence as possible while consolidating the nation's wealth upward. Casually abandon the system of checks and balances to favor totalitarian executive control. And finally create a far-reaching disinformation network to slowly and insidiously convince gullible, ignorant voters that all this damage will actually make their country great again.

Give it a few decades and that nation will crumble.

So what other horrific shit will happen after this book is published? I'll go through the drafts and edits and the stressful process to try to be anonymous, and this admin will have done a thousand new tyrannical things that I wasn't able to include.

FINAL RANT

Maybe the "Don't Tread On Me" crowd will welcome the flimsiest excuse for nationwide martial law imposed by a draft-dodging, veteran-hating traitor.

Maybe the military will fill peaceful blue-city streets under orders to quell the criminal uprising of revolutionaries.

Maybe the admin will finally burn the First Amendment and forbid all criticism of the government, making this book illegal.

Maybe ICE will celebrate an order to start targeting all registered Democrats and outspoken Progressives next.

Maybe they'll have thrown us into a new war with one of our longest standing allies, or maybe they'll keep us in the Middle East under the manufactured threat of WMDs again.

Maybe we'll be the American Empire in a few years.

Maybe he'll be dead.

Regardless, the book *will* miss monumental news. This collection of rants was intended to focus more on the overarching failures of the country's decades of Conservatism, though. We just happen to be living in a pivotal historical moment where America's fascist seeds are sprouting. And Conservatives have been diligently watering.

I know my dad will be gone long before he'll experience the results of his proud selfishness and baffling idiocy. Arguing with him about all this has felt more and more futile as the years go on.

He's lost. Like so many others, he is lost.

His brainwashed hatred of Democrats and Progressives has totally eclipsed any semblance of logic and empathy, and the best he can do to help the country heal is to die. It's quite the bitter truth for many like me, I'm sure.

If the dust ever settles on all of this in a way that leaves America safer and moving forward alongside democracy again, I will want a reckoning the likes of which we haven't seen since Nuremberg.

Every groveling Cabinet member, every corrupt Congressman, every unquestioning ICE agent, every complicit judge, every crooked businessman, and every manipulative mouthpiece of the regime that is trying to destroy us deserves to face real, law-abiding justice.

That is the only outcome with a chance of getting this country back on a path of true progress. But I have no faith in such justice anymore after January 6th. It fled the moment Trump walked free.

Some of you may read all of this book and think, "Man, they should run for office!" I appreciate that, but no. It's not for me. I stammer and stutter when I talk. I have difficulty forming the cohesive sentences necessary for impromptu speeches. I'm too self-conscious for public scrutiny. My charisma is my dump stat.

I enjoyed writing this book, but that very public sort of life isn't for me. I barely even use social media. So thanks, but no thanks.

I said it in the introductory chapter, but I don't imagine this book will succeed anyway. It's just not the type of thing people buy. And that's okay! It wasn't ever really about that. My personality won't let me *not* try to market for its success, but I have low expectations.

If it did make me some money, I'd just use it to cover the costs of publishing this book and to move out of this shithole state.

I know that if people like me leave places like Texas then I'm dooming the state to Republican domination for eternity. I know. This state just isn't safe anymore, y'all. My children need better than Texas. My health needs better than Texas. My sanity needs better than Texas.

And if the country somehow manages to finally split, I want to be on the side with fewer stupid, evil people running the show.

And who knows, maybe this book finds its way through the country, and it ends up on Fox News.

They'd read out the most scathing, out-of-context remarks and cry that Conservatives are being attacked and how free-speech like this book should be illegal.

The cultists would don their Made in China MAGA hats and go review-bomb the book online or ironically buy a bunch of copies to burn.

The bootlicking Reddit mod team of r/Conservative would protect the alternate reality of their "flaired users only" safe space and ban any positive discussion of the book.

The propagandist podcasters would analyze every little sentence so they can attack the whole of Progressivism before hawking their newest alpha-male supplement line.

They could hunt me down, dissolve my anonymity, arrest me on some false charge, deport my very legal citizen ass to Ecuador or maybe put me in their newly renovated Alcatraz. Who knows.

All because my words hurt their fragile little feelings.

Y'all could prove me wrong though! About this *entire* book!

You could fight for truly free and fair democratic voting systems.

You could never again support demagogues and dictators.

You could strive to end poverty and shield both laborers and consumers.

You could take charge in the quest to metaphorically slay our dragons.

You could decree that healthcare is a human right not for profit.

You could uplift our schools and feed our hungry learners.

You could join us as stewards and shepherds of a greener tomorrow.

You could embrace the need for diversity, equity, and inclusion.

You could shift your focus from criminal punishment to criminal reform.

You could confine your religion to a personal practice separate from law.

You could do all of this!

If any American Conservatives actually read this book with any trace of an open mind, I challenge you — I beg you — take your growing pile of "fell for it again" awards and learn something!

Reflect on the heart of my rants and try to grasp the abundant flaws of your policies and your worldview.

Find and foster whatever empathy resides within you.

Peer past the tribalism, the decades of deception, the corrupted influencers, and the misplaced aggression.

Stop letting the leopards devour your face!

Finally open your eyes and see the dripping contempt your leaders hold for you and your peers!

Your elites do not give one shred of a fuck about you and will say whatever bullshit they must to secure your vote. They only want to grow fat and happy and insulated from their intentionally oppressive policies.

That is all that they have ever done, and they will never see you as anything but a tool to be worked to death and food for the dragons.

You must accept and learn from these truths.

Please, help the Progressives work for a better world.

Otherwise you will continue supporting the stupid and evil.

— · ✂ · —

ACKNOWLEDGMENTS

I want to thank my wonderful partner for letting me rant about politics all these years. Even when everything feels like it's going to shit and the world is turning upside down, I know you will stand by my side, helping me tackle the inevitable waves of "stressy depressy".

There's a long road ahead, but I very much look forward to raising those bright, empathetic kiddos with you.

I also want to thank everyone that read this book, regardless of your ideology. It was a lot more work than I anticipated, and I appreciate the support. I hope you got a few hours of entertainment out of it, at least.

I know the print quality isn't great. The "premium" quality print had an unconscionable price tag even when I made zero dollars per sold copy.

You can find clearer, high-resolution versions of my sloppy artwork (for as long as the site I slapped together functions) here:

stupid-evil-or-both.com

To the Progressives — Y'all keep fighting for a better tomorrow.

To the Conservatives — I hope you learned something. Be better.

— . ⚒ . —

www.ingramcontent.com/pod-product-compliance
Lightning Source LLC
Chambersburg PA
CBHW060128130626
46556CB00006B/2276

* 9 7 9 8 9 9 9 9 0 5 8 6 4 *